Haley

Top Secret

Haley's No peeking
(caloud!)

Top ☆ ☆ ☆ ☆ ☆

Top Secret

Haley

Book

Top Secret

A Handbook of Codes, Ciphers, and Secret Writing

Paul B. Janeczko
illustrated by Jenna LaReau

SCHOLASTIC INC.
New York Toronto London Auckland Sydney
Mexico City New Delhi Hong Kong Buenos Aires

ISBN 0-439-87560-9

Text copyright © 2004 by Paul B. Janeczko.
Illustrations copyright © 2004 by Jenna LaReau. All rights reserved.
Published by Scholastic Inc., 557 Broadway, New York, NY 10012,
by arrangement with Candlewick Press. SCHOLASTIC and
associated logos are trademarks and/or registered
trademarks of Scholastic Inc.

12 11 10 9 8 7 6 5 4 3 2 1   6 7 8 9 10 11/0

Printed in the U.S.A.   23

First Scholastic paperback printing, April 2006

The book was typeset in Caecilia.
The illustrations were done in acrylic, charcoal, and pencil.

For Teri Lesesne,
kind and generous lady,
whose heart and spirit are grand

P. B. J.

Contents

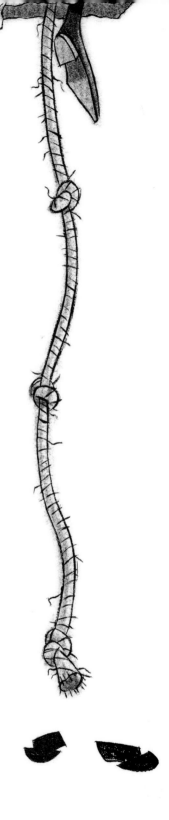

introduction

As long as I can remember, I've been interested in codes and ciphers. There are a lot of reasons. For one thing, I've always enjoyed a good puzzle, whether it's a math puzzle or a word game. I've also been a fan of spy novels and movies. I love all that cloak-and-dagger stuff, all those mysterious meetings in exotic places. And I've been something of a history buff, especially interested in how individuals shaped history. All of these interests find their way into any exploration of codes and ciphers.

I'm sure you have your own reason for picking up this field guide, but I suspect that you're a lot like me. There is something about codes and ciphers—how to make them, how to break them, how they changed history—that fascinates you. Maybe you've dreamed of designing a cipher that is "unbreakable." Or working against time to break a secret code. Or trying to create the perfect invisible ink. If this sounds like you, then this guide is just for you.

This book is about *making* codes and ciphers, not just reading about them. To get the most out of this book, I suggest you create a codemaker's field kit. You might want to think of it as your spy kit, a place where you can store all your tools for codemaking and codebreaking. I suggest you use a shoe box or a plastic storage box. That should give you enough room, at least for starters, to store the cipher tools and codebooks you will make. You can also keep the invisible ink and the pens, toothpicks, and developers that go along with it. By the time you work your way through this book, you will have many things to keep in your field kit.

While you don't need a cloak or a dagger for your field kit, I think it's a good idea for you to have a notebook or journal in which you can keep track of some of the things you will create along the way—things like code names and suitable keywords for a number of different ciphers. The notebook is also the perfect place to work out solutions for intercepted messages and to design the new codes and ciphers you will dream up.

But don't just rely on what you read about in this book to decide what to put in your field kit and in your notebook. Be inventive. Use your imagination to think of other things that can help you as a codemaker and codebreaker.

One of the ways to get new ideas about codes and ciphers is to read books and stories that show how spies carry out their business. I hope you get some ideas from the stories that are scattered throughout the book. They tell about some of the famous codes, codemakers, and codebreakers in history. At the end of this book, I've suggested some other books that will give you even more information about the world of codes and espionage.

Since even a real spy doesn't work alone, making and breaking codes is much more fun if you work with a partner. And it's even more fun if you pick a partner who wants to be inventive. You know the kind of person I mean—someone who is willing to try something clever to make a good code better. Someone who is willing to take chances or makes guesses to break a code.

If you are nuts about codes and ciphers and secret writing, this guide has it all: codes, ciphers, invisible inks, concealment techniques, spy stories, and even a little bit of history (but only the exciting parts). Find a friend and start reading this book and building your codemaker's field kit. The fun has just begun!

AREYAY OUYAY EADYRAY ORFAY AYAY

OPTAY ECRETSAY ISSIONMAY?

Are you ready for a
top Secret mission?

YES!

PART 1
Codemaking

Before we talk about making and breaking codes, we need to realize that most of the time when people talk about making codes and breaking codes, they are not talking about codes at all. They're really talking about ciphers. What's the difference? A **code** is a system where every word or phrase in your message is replaced by another word, phrase, or series of symbols. On the other hand, a **cipher** is a system where every *letter* of your message is replaced by another letter or symbol.

For now, let's stick with codes. For example, you and your partner can make up code words for places in your neighborhood. Your code word for "post office" might be GREEN. Your code word for "playground" might be AWARD.

A code can also be a number. We might say that the code for "post office" is 71715. And the code for "playground" is 71716. Again, the words or numbers themselves don't matter, as long as you and your partner know what they mean.

HOBO SIGNS

Long before there was language as we know it, prehistoric people communicated with pictures. The walls of many ancient caves are covered with *pictographs,* pictures that tell a story. But these ancient people are not the only ones who have communicated with pictures. Another group that used pictographs was hoboes, those men and women who traveled the country, hitching rides on railroad cars.

The life of the hobo could be very dangerous. Railroad police, known by hoboes as "bulls," were always ready to rough up any hobo who dared to take a free ride on a train. Even in cities and towns, people did not always welcome hoboes with open arms, so hoboes needed to stick together to help each other. One of the ways they did this was to develop a secret code—a system of simple, easy-to-read symbols—that offered advice and warnings to other hoboes.

Hoboes drew these symbols on houses or other buildings. Sometimes they left them in "hobo jungles," the spots where they made camp along the way. At right are some examples of the symbols that hoboes used.

Can you think of some hobo signs that might help a traveler passing through your neighborhood? Take another look at the hobo signs and see what new signs you can come up with. Remember to keep them simple and write them in your notebook.

⧄ A GOOD ROAD TO FOLLOW

⧄△ THESE PEOPLE ARE RICH
(TOP HAT + PILE OF GOLD)

VVVV WARNING: BARKING DOGS

/// THIS IS NOT A SAFE PLACE

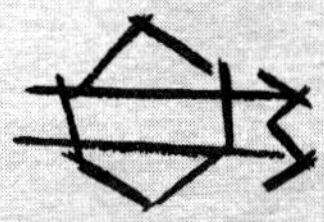

⬦ HIT THE ROAD! BE QUICK!

⬓ A GENTLEMAN LIVES HERE
(TOP HAT)

⬡⬡ POLICE ARE NOT FRIENDLY
TOWARD HOBOES HERE
(HANDCUFFS)

⬦ BE PREPARED TO DEFEND
YOURSELF

⊗ A GOOD PLACE TO HANG OUT

oXo FRESH WATER AND A SAFE
CAMPSITE

Not all codes are secret. We encounter nonsecret codes every day. One such code is on every piece of mail: the **Zip Code!** (Did you catch that: Zip *Code*?) Officially known as the Zone Improvement Plan, the Zip Code was first used on July 1, 1963, to speed the accurate delivery of mail. Each number in a Zip Code has a purpose. The first digit of a five-digit Zip Code represents one of ten service areas of the country, starting with 0 for the Northeast to 9 on the West Coast. The next two digits represent Sectional Center Facilities (SCFs) within the larger service areas. The final two digits represent a delivery unit of the SCF. Some areas now use a Zip + 4 system in which the final four digits represent a number of locations that a mail carrier delivers to.

Speaking of mail, you may also have noticed the short lines that are printed on the bottom edge of an envelope below the address. This is a **bar code** for the Zip Code. Different patterns of vertical bars stand for the digits 0 to 9, so a mail-sorting computer can read them and then direct that piece of mail to the proper place.

You don't have to look at your mail to see a bar code. Just about anything you buy in a store, from a CD to a bag of dog food, has a bar code on it; this is the **UPC**, or **Universal Product Code**. When you buy something, the computer in the cash register takes note of its bar code. This helps retailers keep track of their inventory.

If you'd like to see another way that nonsecret codes are part of your life, just flip to the back cover of this book. You will see another bar code, above which you will see a number; this is the book's **ISBN**, or **International Standard Book Number**, which is different for every book. Each publisher is allotted one or more prefixes, each made up of a single digit, a dash, several more digits, and another dash. The numbers that follow the prefix are those that designate a specific book. And as you can see, this is a simple way for both booksellers and publishers to keep track of sales. Also, if you know the ISBN of a book, that makes it a breeze to order it in your local bookstore.

Today's Zip Codes and bar codes are a far cry from the original very secret codes that were developed in the 1300s. The political situation at the time in Europe made it necessary for some countries to keep secret the names of some important persons; a list of code words, called a **nomenclator**, was developed to disguise the names of

EVERYDAY

ICTOGRAPHS

You may not realize it, but you come face to face with pictographs every day. When you ride down the highway or through city streets, you see pictographs on blue road signs. Do you recognize these "nonsecret" codes?

These signs rely on a symbol, not words, to tell us that we are near a a telephone, hospital, gas station, and a restaurant. No matter where you travel in this country, you will see the same signs. Try to figure out what these code signs mean:

Answers on page 132.

Can you think up some pictographs that you and a partner can use to indicate certain places? You can include symbols for places and people at your school or in your neighborhood. Keep your symbols simple so they will be easy to draw.

those people. When a message was sent, the only words in code were the names that needed to be kept secret.

With time, the need to keep more and more secrets grew. As that need grew, the number of nomenclators grew. Originally, these lists were kept on large sheets of parchment, but as the need to keep secrets became more urgent, it became unwise to leave sheets of parchment lying around for prying eyes to look at. Covers were then put on the nomenclators, and that gave us our first codebooks.

The world of codes changed even more in 1844 when Samuel F. B. Morse developed his **Morse code**, a system of short and long signals representing letters and numbers that could be sent quickly over the telegraph. Then, in 1866, the transatlantic cable was completed, linking communication between the United States and Europe. The combination of Morse code and the completion of the transatlantic cable revolutionized trade and commerce and gave rise to even more commercial codes. People who ran businesses realized that they could save money on their cabled messages by cutting down on the number of words they sent. So they developed codes. Instead of sending "Your order has been shipped," they could simply send, for example, ASDFG. No connection between the message and the five-letter code was necessary. Speed and accuracy were most important when businesses designed their codebooks.

Secret Codes

Every good secret agent needs a wide array of techniques and tricks. The more code and cipher systems you master, the easier it will be for you to switch from one to another as the situation dictates. After you have read through this section and tried your hand at making these codes and ciphers, you might settle on a handful that you like better than the others. Just remember one thing: don't use one system for too long. The longer you stick with one system, the greater the chances that your adversary might pick up the patterns in your messages and break your system.

There are two different types of codes: one-part and two-part. In the one-part code, the **plaintext**, or the words that you want to keep secret, *and* their code equivalents are in alphabetical (by letter) or sequential (by number) order. This means that you only need one codebook to send or receive a message because all the code and plaintext words are in order and easy to find. For example, a one-part code might look like this in a codebook:

```
GABAA — game after school
GABCD — game at park
GABEF — game at school
GABHJ — game begins at seven
GABLM — game canceled
GABPQ — game moved back one hour
GABST — game tomorrow
```

You can see that both the code and the plaintext phrases are in alphabetical order. This organized arrangement allows you to encode and decode a message with this single codebook.

In a two-part code, you actually have *two separate* codebooks. In the *encoding* codebook, the plaintext words are in alphabetical order (because when you are encoding a message, you need to easily find the word that you will be sending), but the codes listed next to them are random. So the encoding book for a two-part code might look like this:

BEACH	11
BICYCLE	55
LIBRARY	22
NOTEBOOK	66
PARK	88
SCHOOL	77
STORE	33
TREE HOUSE	44

In the *decoding* codebook, the *codes* are in sequential order and the plaintext equivalents are random. So the decoding book for this two-part code would look like this:

When you create a two-part code, each part should be kept in its own book. So, in order to encode *and* decode, you and a partner will each need to have both books. The reason for this goes back in history; a spy working in the field often merely encoded messages to send to his contact, so there was no need for him to have the decoding part, lessening the chance that the code could fall into enemy hands.

The only real advantage of using a code rather than a cipher is that it is much easier to encode and decode a message using a code, especially a two-part code, because all you need to do is find the words you need on a systematic list. This takes less time than enciphering each letter of a message. For example, if you wanted to meet your friend in front of the library, all you would need to do is look up "library" in your codebook and send her its code.

Despite the benefits, there are disadvantages to using codebooks. They can be large and difficult to transport. Also they can be lost, stolen, or copied, which will put your operation in jeopardy. It's much easier to create a new cipher than to create an entire new codebook. Another disadvantage of a codebook is that it takes a lot of time to make a good one because you have to include all the words that you might want to use in your messages.

And, of course, you always need to have your codebook near you when you get a message. A cipher system—usually called a "paper and pencil" system—can be easily committed to memory, with no need of a bulky codebook close at hand.

With a little work and a lot of fun, you can make your own one-part codebook. Get together with your partner and make up a list of all the words that you think you will need to use in your communications. Make sure you include the names of people, places, and things that are important. You might also include days of the week, numbers (which can be used to show meeting times, for example), and adjectives. After you have decided on

A NEW CODE FOR A NEW NATION

After the Revolutionary War, it was important for the statesmen of the new nation to send secret messages. This meant they had to improve on the codes they had used during the war.

In 1781 Robert R. Livingston, the U.S. secretary of state, created a form that listed the numbers 1 to 1,700 along with an alphabetical list of letters, syllables, and words that might be needed in diplomatic communications. American diplomats used this system, and similar ones, to assign numbers to the plaintext in a variety of ways. A particular set of equivalents might be used for a week or a month, and then a new set would be created. Of course, everyone involved with sending and receiving secret messages needed to know how and when the equivalents were being changed — but the numbered chart gave them the chance to easily change their code at will, a smart practice for all codemakers.

James Madison, a member of the new House of Representatives, and Thomas Jefferson, the foreign minister to France, used Livingston's sheet for about eight years, beginning in 1785. Despite the careful system, things did not always work smoothly. A story is told of how Madison found himself on vacation when he received a partially encoded message from Jefferson: "We have decided unanimously to 130 . . . interest if they do not 510 . . . to the 636." The problem was that Madison had left the key to the code in his office in Philadelphia!

all the words you will include in your codebook, you need to put them in alphabetical order—that way you will be able to easily find the words you want to use in your message.

Next, you need to decide what you are going to use for codes. Assign a code for every word on your plaintext list. They could be numbers; in fact, numbers can be a good way to go with your first codebook because they fall into a natural sequence. I suggest that you use three- or four-digit numbers. Whether you use numbers or words for your codes, put them in numerical sequence or alphabetical order.

Once you have all the plaintext words you think you are going to need and all the code words for them, you have created a one-part codebook. And since both the plaintext and code words are in sequential order, this type of codebook should serve you and your partner quite well for encoding and decoding messages.

As I've mentioned, one of the drawbacks of a codebook is that it can be lost or stolen, so you have to make sure that you hide yours where it won't be discovered. You don't want it falling into the wrong hands!

However, you already have a codebook in your home right now and didn't even know it. Where is it? Well, look around your room. Do you see any books? If you do, almost any of them can be a codebook.

Book Code

Any novel or textbook can be a codebook. All you need to do is find in the book the words you want to include in your message. Then you need to create a system to communicate those words to your partner. The usual method is to give the location of the word by writing out the number of the page on which the word is found, followed by the number of the line on which the word is found, and then a number for the place of that word in the line. For example, let's suppose that the word PLAY is the fifth word in the seventeenth line on page 223 of *A Tale of Two Cities*, your codebook. The code word for PLAY would be 2231705. In other words:

223 for the page number

17 for the line in which the word
appears on that page

05 for the position of that word on that line

You should set up your book code with the understanding that the first three digits will be the page number, the next two digits will be the line, and the last two digits will be the position in the line. Therefore, every code word will be a seven-digit

"word." Notice that I stuck in a zero before the five to keep that part of the code word a two-digit number. You'd do the same thing, if necessary, for the page number and the line number.

If this system is going to work for you and your partner, you must make sure that you and she will be using the exact same edition of the same book. Otherwise, your code words will not work out. One of the advantages of this system is that you can change the book whenever you want, thereby making your encoded messages more difficult to break.

● Dictionary Code

The dictionary has been the most popular book that agents have used to create a book code. But since dictionaries are usually printed in two columns, you need to adjust the formula for your code word a bit. Start with the page number, supplying zeros when necessary to make this a three-digit number. Then you need to include an indicator for the left or right column; for example, you could use 1 for the left and 2 for the right. The final two digits would indicate the position of your word in that column. So, if the word CAT was the fifteenth word in the left-hand column on page 45, you might write it as 045115. Using this dictionary system, every code word should have six digits in it.

Advanced Technique

You can also create a simple dictionary code based on one that was used in a scandal surrounding the presidential election of 1876. You simply find the word you want to use in a dictionary and note its position on the page. Then you move four pages toward the front of the dictionary and use the word on that page that is in the same position as the word you want to send.

For example, in my dictionary, the word SCANDAL is word nineteen on page 1197. To encode that word, look for the nineteenth word on page 1193, which happens to be SATURATE. Then write that word as part of your secret message. Clever, don't you think?

To decode a message sent as SATURATE, you simply reverse the process: find SATU-RATE, count its position on the page, then move ahead four pages and find the nineteenth word on that page.

◉ Codetalking

Some codes work better when they are spoken. In fact, during both World Wars, the United States used Native Americans as "codetalkers."

The number of these codetalkers rose from thirty at the beginning of World War II to more than four hundred by the end of the war. They originally served in the Pacific, but before too long, Native Americans were serving as battlefield "codetalkers" in North Africa and Europe. These soldiers—from tribes like the Choctaw, Comanche, Navaho, and Hopi—used their tribal languages to transmit secret messages from field telephones.

Native American languages are well suited for this sort of secret activity. The languages are very difficult to learn and speak correctly. Like other languages they rely on vocabulary, but these Native American languages are also affected by voice inflection and space between words. This last feature made it very difficult for a nonspeaker to learn the language well enough to fool—or even communicate with—a true speaker. For this reason, Native American codetalkers usually worked in pairs. And ultimately, these Native American codes have become known as some of the few unbreakable codes in history.

● Pig Latin

Other spoken codes seem to have originated on the playgrounds in Europe and England. Pig Latin, which has nothing to do with pigs or Latin, is simple, and easy to master. Here are the rules:

1. If a word begins with vowel, you simply add YAY to the end of the word. For example, EAR becomes EARYAY, OPEN becomes OPENYAY, and APE becomes APEYAY.

2. If a word begins with a consonant, you move it to the end of the word and add AY. If the initial consonant sound is made up of two letters, like TH and CH, you move both to the end of the word and add AY. So, CHIN becomes INCHAY, BASEBALL becomes ASEBALLBAY, and TRUNK becomes UNKTRAY.

Like most spoken codes, if pig Latin is written out, it doesn't fool a codebreaker for very long. However, when it is spoken precisely and *quickly*, it can be an effective code.

PRACTICE!

Translate these Pig Latin words into English:

ODECAY

ATHAY

INKWAY

IGPAY

UPIDSTAY

Encode this sentence into Pig Latin:

THE GAME WILL START AT SIX.

Answers on page 132.

• Turkish Irish

Turkish Irish is another schoolyard game that has lasted for a long time. You simply put AB *before* each vowel in a word. When you have two vowels together in a word, like in REACH or FEET, you add your syllable *before* the first vowel. So, CLOCK becomes CLABOCK, BIKE becomes BABIKE, and FEET becomes FABEET. Again, this is a code system that works best when you speak your messages quickly.

You can see that some of the spoken codes can easily get out of hand and be quite comical. You can even try to come up with your own! But regardless of which spoken code you use, the key to its success is how well you speak it. And that takes practice.

ᴋᴏᴛ ᴡᴏ̜ ɪᴍs ᴏᴘ **Ciphers** ɢᴢx ᴊ ʙɴʏᴀᴄᴏ

Essentially, there are two types of ciphers: substitution and transposition. The difference between them is quite simple. In a **substitution cipher**, you substitute one symbol for every letter in the plaintext. For example, I could substitute the numbers 1 to 26 for the letters of the alphabet. In such a system, HELP would be enciphered as 8-5-12-16. In a **transposition cipher**, you transpose or rearrange the positions of the letters. For example, I could transpose HELP to read PLEH. My system was to simply write the word backward. In this section you will learn a number of true transposition systems to encipher longer messages.

Let's take a look at a simple transposition. If my message is GET OUT NOW, I might encipher that as TEG TUO WON. No doubt you noticed that I simply wrote each word in reverse order. Of course, this simple system won't fool any serious code-breaker for very long, but there are other transposition systems that are devilishly clever.

In addition, transposition of longer sentences affords an

astronomical number of possible combinations. For example, let's take a simple sentence of thirty-five letters: MAKING CODES AND CIPHERS CAN BE LOTS OF FUN. From those letters you can make 50,000,000,000,000,000,000,000,000,000 different combinations. How many is that? Well, one mathematician figures it this way: if one person could check one combination per second, and if all the people in the world worked twenty-four hours a day, it would take more than a thousand times the lifetime of the universe to check all the possibilities. Now *that's* a lot of possibilities!

Substitution and transposition cipher systems both have their advantages and disadvantages. Substitution ciphers are easier to break, but transposition ciphers are not as easy to use. As you will see later, when I explain how to break a secret message, it is important to recognize both systems and know how each operates.

Before we get started learning about ciphers, let me say a few words about terms. As you know, a code replaces plaintext words with words or phrases, while a cipher replaces each letter in a plaintext with a cipher letter. So when you make a cipher, you are not, technically speaking, codemaking—you are enciphering. And when you solve a cipher message, you are not codebreaking—you are deciphering. However, the terms "codemaking" and "codebreaking" have come to be used more generally to include working with ciphers as well as codes.

Caesar Cipher

Probably the granddaddy of all simple substitution ciphers was used by Roman Emperor Julius Caesar (100–44 B.C.), although some historians feel that this cipher was in use long before Caesar was born. As he roamed far and wide across his vast empire, Caesar needed a way to make sure that if any of his messages fell into enemy hands, his secret plans would remain safe. To disguise his messages, Caesar simply shifted the alphabet three places, giving him:

PLAIN: A B C D E F G H I J K L M N O P Q R S T U V W X Y Z
CIPHER: X Y Z A B C D E F G H I J K L M N O P Q R S T U V W

So, if you wanted to send this message: MEETING TOMORROW AT STATION, you would write it as JBBQFKD QLJLOOLT XQ PQX-QFLK. Nothing to it!

PRACTICE!

Use the Caesar cipher on these messages:

Encipher these messages:

    1. DELIVERY OF SUPPLIES DELAYED.

    2. MEET AGENT IN FRONT OF POST OFFICE.

Decipher these messages:

    1. OBJBJYBO QL ZEXKDB VLRO AFPDRFPB.

    2. X DLLA XDBKQ HBBMP EBO ZLLI.

Answers on page 132.

● St. Cyr Slide

If you are like a lot of other codemakers, you might be wondering why Caesar shifted the alphabet three places and let it go at that. What would it be like, you might wonder, if you were able to shift the alphabet as many places as you wish? Well, your question was answered in the 1850s at the French national military academy in St. Cyr, where cryptographers developed a slide device that became known as the **St. Cyr slide**. With a little bit of patience and a few simple tools, you can make your own St. Cyr slide.

To begin, cut a strip of paper about a half-inch wide and long enough for you to print the alphabet twice, one right after the other. The other part of the slide is a file card. Somewhere near the middle of the card, print the alphabet in its normal sequence. Be careful that the letters of the alphabet you print on the card are about the same size as the letters on the strip of paper because you will need to line up the letters on the strip directly under the letters on the card. Use a computer to type it and print it out if you can. Next, below the ends of the alphabet on the card, carefully cut two slits a bit wider than the strip of letters. From behind the card, slide the strip through one of the slits, pull it across the card, and then slide it through the other slit. When you are finished, your St. Cyr slide should look like this:

To encipher a message, slide the strip so the letter of your choice is below the A. Next, find the plaintext letter on the card and use the letter directly below it on the strip in your secret message. So, following the example in the illustration (in which K is lined up under A), you would encipher SUNNY WEATHER as CEXXI GOKDROB.

When you are trying to decipher a message, you reverse the process: line up the letter you and your partner have chosen under the A, find the enciphered letter on the strip, then look for the plaintext letter directly above it.

PRACTICE!

Use the St. Cyr slide pictured on page 29 on these messages:

Encipher:

    1. I LIKE TO WRITE CIPHERS.

    2. PRACTICE YOUR CODES AND CIPHERS.

Decipher:

    1. MYNOC RKFO MRKXQON RSCDYBI.

    2. LOGKBO YP CZSOC.

Answers on page 132.

Advanced Technique

You probably noticed that all the alphabets in the Caesar cipher and the St. Cyr slide are in the normal order. This does not always have to be the case. You could, for example, write the alphabets on the slide in reverse order. You can do the same thing with the alphabet on the card. Or you can use the numbers 1 to 26 for the letters of the alphabets on the slide. You can use odd numbers. Even numbers. Or you can use numbers in reverse order. You must, however, make sure that your strip alphabets go in the same direction—which means no random alphabets. Were you to use random alphabets, you could easily have the same cipher letter lining up under two different plaintext letters.

Also, you do not have to use letters or numbers on your slide. You can use symbols for each letter of the alphabet. One caution, however: if you use symbols on your St. Cyr slide, like those shown on the next few pages, make sure you give yourself enough space on the card and slide so that the plaintext alphabet and your symbols on the card line up. You may, in fact, need a larger slide and card.

Substitution Ciphers in Literature

One of the most famous students of cryptography was American writer and poet Edgar Allan Poe (1809–1849). In addition to stories such as "The Tell-Tale Heart" and "The Fall of the House of Usher," Poe also wrote "A Few Words on Secret Writing," an essay in which he offered the following substitution cipher:

) shall stand for a				′ " " " n
(" " " b				† " " " o
— " " " c				‡ " " " p
* " " " d				¶ " " " q
. " " " e				☞ " " " r
, " " " f				] " " " s
; " " " g				[" " " t
: " " " h				£ " " " u or v
? " " " i or j				$ " " " w
! " " " k				¿ " " " x
& " " " l				¡ " " " y
0 " " " m				☜ ¶ " " z

Poe even made a cipher an important part of his short story "The Gold Bug." In that story, the main character, a man named LeGrand, must decipher a message in the hope that it will lead him to Captain Kidd's buried treasure.

Here is the message:

53‡‡†305))6*;4826)4‡.)4‡);806*;48†8¶60))85;;]8*;:‡*
8†83(88)5*†;46(;88*96*?;8)*‡(;485);5*†2:*‡(;4956*2(5
—4)8¶8;4069285);)6†8)4‡‡;1(‡9;48081;8:8‡1;48†8
5;4)485†528806*81(‡9;48;(88;4(‡?34;48)4‡;161;:188;‡?;

In "The Adventure of the *Gloria Scott*" by Sir Arthur Conan Doyle, Sherlock Holmes puts his skills of deduction to work to break a null cipher. Holmes and Dr. Watson, his ever-faithful sidekick, come up against another cipher in "The Adventure of the Dancing Men." The duo must deal with a series of pictographic messages, which turn out to be a simple substitution cipher. Here is one of the messages:

Be sure to check out these stories from your local library — in particular, you can learn just how LeGrand and Sherlock Holmes apply some of the rules of codebreaking to solve these infamous ciphers. (And of course, you can check the back of this book for the solutions!)

Answers on page 133.

THE Shadow's CIPHER

"The Shadow," a very popular crime fighter in books and in his own radio shows during the 1930s, used an ingenious system to send his secret messages. Here's what his cipher alphabet looked like:

Keyboard Cipher

If you have access to a computer at school or at home, you can easily turn the keyboard into a cipher machine. After all, it has the alphabet printed on it, right? All you need to do is find a system that can help you send secret messages with it. Take a look at this secret message: XLKK NW LA AIIB LA OIAAUVKW.

Notice the four numbered symbols at the bottom of the chart. Those are not ciphers for the numbers 1–4. They show your partner the position you held the paper in when the cipher message was written and, therefore, tell her how to hold the paper when she tries to decipher the message.

For example, the first symbol, with that little line pointing straight up, tells your partner that you had your sheet of paper in the normal position when you wrote the cipher. So, to decipher it, she should hold the paper in the normal fashion. However, the next symbol, with the little line at the 3 o'clock position, means that you turned your paper one turn to the right when you wrote the message. So when you partner tries to decipher this message, she must turn the paper to the right. Because these symbols are in circles, they can mean different things, depending on how the page is held.

Doesn't make any sense, does it? That's because I used the letter immediately to the left of the letter I wanted to use in my message: CALL ME AS SOON AS POSSIBLE. Since the A is the last letter on the left of the middle row, I had to "wrap around" to the other end of that same row. That's where the L's come from.

Remember that when you decipher a message, you need to reverse the process you used to encipher a message. So, in this case, to find the plaintext, you need to look for the letter that is to the right of the cipher letter.

PRACTICE!

Decipher this message, using the letters that are to the right of each letter. Don't forget about the wraparound!

AOUWA BWWS RI VW XLEWDYK.

Answer on page 133.

● Morse Code

If you have a flashlight in the house, you have another piece of equipment that can help you send secret messages. You might, in fact, want to include a pocket flashlight in your field kit. With some practice, you can use the flashlight to send messages using **Morse code** (which, you can see, is really a cipher—because each letter in a message is represented by a single set of dots and dashes). The flashlight is especially helpful for sending messages over a distance at night.

Here is Morse code:

A	•—	N	—•	1	•————	Ñ	——•——
B	—•••	O	———	2	••———	Ö	———•
C	—•—•	P	•——•	3	•••——	Ü	••——
D	—••	Q	——•—	4	••••—	,	••—••
E	•	R	•—•	5	•••••	.	•—•—•—
F	••—•	S	•••	6	—••••	?	••——••
G	——•	T	—	7	——•••	;	—•—•—
H	••••	U	••—	8	———••	:	———•••
I	••	V	•••—	9	————•	/	—••—•
J	•———	W	•——	0	—————	-	—••••—
K	—•—	X	—••—	Á	•——•—	'	•————•
L	•—••	Y	—•——	Ä	•—•—	()	—•——•—
M	——	Z	——••	É	••—••	_	••——•—

If I was to encipher ROSIE, the name of my dog, it would look like this: •—• ——— ••• •• •. Notice that the O and the S in her name are found in the international distress signal: SOS ••• ——— •••. If you take a close look at the Morse code table above, you might also notice that the most common letters in the English language, like E and T, have the shortest Morse code letters.

PRACTICE!

Use Morse code to encipher your name and the names of a couple of your friends. Then try to decipher this message:

-- --- •-• ••• • / -•-• --- -•• • / •• ••• /

•-• • •- •-•• •-•• -•-- / •- / -•-• •• •--• •••• • •-•. /

Answer on page 133.

● Semaphore

Another cipher system that can be used over distances is **semaphore**, a system that uses the position of two flags to represent letters. Here is the semaphore alphabet:

A   B   C   D   E   F   G

H   I   J   K   L   M   N

O   P   Q   R   S   T   U

V   W   X   Y   Z

Of course, you don't need flags to send a semaphore message. What's important is the position of the arms. You could, for example, raise your arms in the Y position to signal someone on the other side of the cafeteria that the answer to her question is yes.

With a little imagination, the semaphore system can be adapted to be used as a written system of secret writing. If you forget about the flags and picture the arms as the hands of a clock, you can see that each letter will have a streamlined "semaphore" equivalent:

Now you can see how these symbols make up a cipher system that you can use for secret writing. (You can use these symbols on your St. Cyr slide.) Here is how I would write my first name: ⌐⅄∨⁄. Before you try your hand at deciphering a couple of messages, why don't you and your partner try to encipher a few words—like the names of the days of the week or your favorite sports teams—and check the accuracy of each other's work.

PRACTICE!

Use the modified semaphore alphabet to decipher this message:

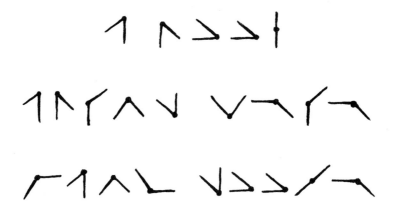

Answer on page 133.

Pigpen Cipher

The pigpen cipher has been around for a long time. Some people think that it was originally used eight hundred years ago during the Crusades. For some reason, it wasn't used much after that

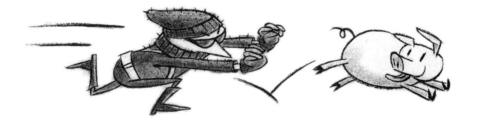

until the 1700s, when it was adopted by a secret society called the Freemasons. For this reason, the pigpen cipher is also referred to as the Freemason cipher. It surfaced again during the American Civil War when a postal inspector found the odd symbols of the cipher in a letter addressed to a man suspected of being a spy for the Confederacy. Here's what the pigpen cipher looks like:

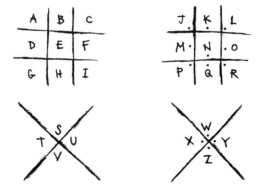

To encipher a message using the pigpen cipher, simply use that part of each drawing that corresponds to the letters in the message you want to encipher. For example, if I wanted to encipher MAINE, it would look like this:

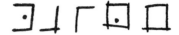

● Rosicrucian Cipher

A cipher system that is similar to the pigpen cipher is the **Rosicrucian cipher,** which uses a single grid with nine parts to it:

It works much the same way as the pigpen cipher works, but every cipher figure includes an important dot. For example, the first three letters of the alphabet would look like this:

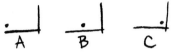

Notice how these three figures are quite similar. It is the placement of the dot that makes such a big difference. The dot indicates whether you mean the letter to the left, in the center, or to the right in the figure. Here's how MAINE would be enciphered in the Rosicrucian cipher:

While this system is more compact than the pigpen cipher, it relies on the position of the dots to indicate the correct letter. A few dots written carelessly in haste can make a secret message more difficult to decipher.

PRACTICE!

Here is a message to decipher using the Rosicrucian cipher:

Answer on page 133.

Substitution Ciphers in History

This substitution cipher was attributed to Charlemagne, who ruled in the eighth and ninth centuries. He relied on this substitution cipher when he communicated with his generals spread across his vast kingdom.

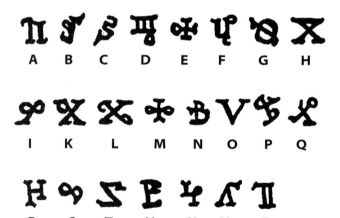

(Note that there is no J, V, or W — those letters weren't part of the alphabet back then.)

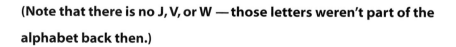

COUSIN MARY

Another European ruler to use a substitution cipher was Mary Queen of Scots. In fact, it was the discovery and deciphering of this system by her enemies that caused her to lose her head to the executioner when she was convicted of plotting to overthrow Queen Elizabeth.

A B C D E F GH IJ K LM N O P Q R S T U V W X Y Z
AND AS BY FOR
MARY
STUART

Sir Francis Walsingham, Elizabeth's master spy, tricked Mary into putting her intentions in writing, which he later used against her.

● Date Shift Cipher

One other way to send a secret message is the **date shift cipher**. First, pick a date, any date. I'll use Steven Spielberg's birthday: December 18, 1946. Next I'll write out that date using numbers and slash marks: 12/18/46. Finally, I will get rid of the slashes, leaving me with a six-digit number that I will use to encipher my message: 121846. (For the first nine months of the year, simply put a zero before the number of that month, making January 01, February 02, and so on. You can do the same thing for the first nine days of the month.) For a message, let's use I ENJOY THE MOVIES OF STEVEN SPIELBERG. Under the message I will write my six-digit number over and over until I come to the end:

```
I   ENJOY   THE   MOVIES   OF   STEVEN   SPIELBERG
1   21846   121   846121   84   612184   612184612
```

To help you encipher this message, write out the alphabet from left to right. Now shift each letter of the plaintext by the number of spaces indicated by the number below it. The letter I shifts one space, making it J; E shifts two spaces, making it G; and so on until you have finished enciphering. Note that Y shifts 6 spaces, causing you to wrap around back to the beginning of the alphabet, landing at E. Your final message would be

J GORSE UJF USBJGT WJ YUGWMR YQKFTFKSI.

This system has the same advantage of the keyword cipher: you can change your key as often as you wish. Just make sure that you and your partner agree on the system that you will use when it is time to change the date. The date shift cipher has an added advantage: it is fairly random, so a letter in the plaintext might be enciphered several different ways. Take a look at the enciphered message above. There are seven E's in the message, but how many different letters stand for those E's?

To decipher a date shift cipher, as with the other substitutions, you simply reverse the process. In other words, above the letters of your message, you write in the date shift numbers. Then you move to the letter than many places *before* the letter in the message.

PRACTICE!

Using the birth date of William Shakespeare, April 23, 1564 (or 04/23/64), encipher this message:

READING POETRY IS GREAT FUN.

Answer on page 133.

All the substitution systems I have described so far have used one symbol to correspond to each letter in the plaintext. But there are a number of substitution systems that are **multilateral**. In other words, they use two symbols to stand for each letter in the plaintext. These systems use a matrix or chart to help with enciphering.

● Greek Square Cipher

The earliest of multilateral systems was developed by Polybius, a historian and cryptographer in ancient Greece. Nearly 2,200 years ago, he invented the device that became known as the **Polybius checkerboard**, or, more simply, the **Greek square**. Each letter in the alphabet has a two-number equivalent based on its position on his matrix:

	1	2	3	4	5
1	A	B	C	D	E
2	F	G	H	IJ	K
3	L	M	N	O	P
4	Q	R	S	T	U
5	V	W	X	Y	Z

NOTE:

As there are twenty-five spaces in the checkerboard and twenty-six letters in the alphabet, the letters I and J occupy the same space and are enciphered in the same way. Your partner should be able to tell which letter you mean based on the rest of your deciphered message.

To encipher a message, you find the letter you want to encipher. Let's use M. First, you need to find the number of the row that M is in: 3. Then find the column it's in: 2. So, the cipher for M would be 32. Here's how you'd encipher the word MATRIX:

letter	row	column	cipher text
M	3	2	32
A	1	1	11
T	4	4	44
R	4	2	42
I	2	4	24
X	5	3	53

So, MATRIX would be enciphered as 32 11 44 42 24 53, or 321144422453. Obviously, your secret message will be twice as long as your plaintext; that is one of the disadvantages of a multilateral cipher system.

PRACTICE!

Decipher these words using the Greek square:

1. 352442114415
2. 13231513251542123411421

Answers on page 134.

Thomas Jefferson's Cipher Wheel

Thomas Jefferson (1743–1826) was a man of great accomplishments. Yet not many people realize that he was responsible for creating the *cipher wheel*, an enciphering device that was the model for a device used by the American military nearly a century later. Jefferson's cipher wheel was really a series of thirty-six wheels or disks that were about two inches in diameter and had a six-inch circumference. Each wheel was about a quarter-inch thick with a random alphabet printed along the edge. These wheels were stacked up and held together by a metal rod that ran through the center of each wheel. A device like a wing nut was tightened at the ends to keep the wheels in place.

Using Jefferson's cipher wheel was quite easy. Suppose you wanted to send this message: SUPPLIES DELAYED ONE HOUR. You would arrange the wheels so that you could read your message on one of the lines of letters. To encipher that message, you would simply send *any other* line of letters. When your partner received this string of meaningless letters, she would simply arrange her wheels to show that string, then look over the other wheels until she came across the one line of letters that made sense.

● Greek Skytale

While a substitution cipher relies on substituting one letter or symbol for each letter in your message, a **transposition cipher** requires that you rearrange, or transpose, the letters that are already in your message. A successful transposition system follows a pattern that sender and receiver can use quickly and accurately.

Once again we turn to the Greeks when we want to see the earliest transposition cipher. A general in ancient Sparta created the *skytale* (rhymes with "Italy") to hide his message. He carefully wrapped a narrow strip of animal hide around a staff that he usually carried with him. Then he wrote his message along the hide, turning the staff every time he needed to write a new line of his message. Anyone who looked at the wrapped hide would easily see the message. But when he unwrapped the hide, it showed merely a string of meaningless letters. He gave that strip to a servant, who may have worn it as a belt until he delivered it to another general. He carefully wrapped it around a staff that was exactly as thick as the original, and he could easily read the secret message!

Even though you are not a battle-hardened general in the Spartan army, you can easily make your own *skytale*.

You will need a pencil and a strip of paper. I suggest you use a basic yellow pencil that has six flat sides, which will make it easier to write your message. Make sure that you and your partner use exactly the same type of pencils—otherwise, the letters will not line up correctly. Next, cut up a sheet of composition paper along the blue lines.

Carefully wrap the strip of paper—about a half-inch wide—around the pencil in a spiral fashion. Once you have your paper properly wrapped, you might want to fasten each end with a bit of clear tape, which will allow you to write your message without worrying about the strip of paper unfurling.

Now pick any flat side of your pencil and carefully print one letter of your message in each open space along the length of the pencil. When you get to the end of the pencil and you still have more to write, simply give your pencil a slight turn and continue your message on the next flat side of the pencil. Your *skytale* should look something like this:

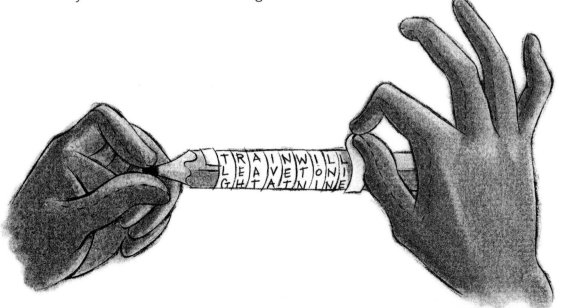

When you have finished writing your secret message, remove the paper from the pencil, and you will see a strip of meaningless letters! If it doesn't look quite right, don't worry about it. You probably just need to practice wrapping the strip around the pencil. To decipher this message, your partner needs only to wrap the strip around an identical pencil and your message should be clear for her to read. Try it!

● Rail Fence Cipher

Another simple transposition cipher is called the **rail fence cipher,** and it dates back to the Civil War. It is called the rail fence because it uses the pattern of a split-rail fence to help in transposing the letters in a message. If you have seen pictures of the split-rail fences that dotted the American countryside in the nineteenth century, you remember how they followed a zigzag pattern. If you looked at such a fence from above, it would look like this:

You will need to keep that pattern in mind as you work on this cipher.

To show you how to write a rail fence cipher, let's use this as our secret message: DO NOT DELAY IN ESCAPING. The first step in enciphering that message would be to write it out in a zigzag fashion like the illustration below. I suggest that you actually draw in the zigzag line to help you move smoothly from letter to letter.

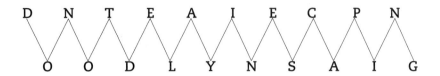

The next step is to write out the letters in the top row as one "word" and the letters in the bottom row as another "word": DNTEAIECPN OODLYNSAIG. That is your secret message. Your partner will decipher the message by writing half the letters along a top row, the second half along a bottom row shifted slightly to the right. She can then draw in the zigzag fence line, and your message will be revealed!

PRACTICE!

Decipher this rail fence cipher message:

1. EGRLAPESDIHR DAALNOUECPES.

Answer on page 134.

Advanced Technique

Now that you know the basics of the rail fence cipher, you might want to think about some variations that you can use to make your messages as secret as possible. One variation is to break your enciphered message into shorter "words" and then write each "word" backward. For example, DNTEAIECPN OODLYNSAIG, from page 55, would become DNTEA IECPN OODLY NSAIG, which would then become AETND NPCEI YLDOO GIASN.

Can you think of other variations of the rail fence cipher that might prove interesting? Play around with some ideas with your partner and write the best ones in your notebook. And remember: always make sure your partner knows which variation you are using.

● Route Transposition Cipher

The most common kind of transposition cipher is called a **route transposition** because your message follows a route or path in a grid. The grid will be a square or a rectangle and is made of small boxes, each containing a letter of your message. Let me give you an example. This time we will use this message: ESCAPE NOW BEFORE ALL IS LOST. This message has twenty-four letters in it, so we can use a square 5 x 5 grid or a rectangular 3 x 8 or 4 x 6 grid. I'll use the square.

On my graph paper I mark off a 5 x 5 grid. Then I write out my message, one letter per box, starting in the upper left-hand corner and going from top to bottom in each column in succession. So my grid now looks like the one pictured below (with a J added as a null to fill out the twenty-five boxes).

To encipher your message, you simply write out the words in the rows of the grid, starting at the top and moving down the grid. Our enciphered message is: EEEAL SNFLO COOLS AWRIT PBESJ. Isn't that easy?

If I had chosen to use a 3 x 8 grid, it would look like this:

And the message would be enciphered like this: EWL SBL CEI AFS POL ERO NES OAT. You can see that changing the shape of the grid changes the enciphered message dramatically. In addition to these two shapes, I could have used grids of 8 x 3, 4 x 6, 6 x 4, 2 x 12, or 12 x 2.

Don't forget: Each time you use this type of cipher system, you and your partner need to agree on the size and shape of your grid and on the starting point and route within the grid. Otherwise, at least one of you is going to be very frustrated!

You are now ready to send and receive secret messages using the many variations that substitution and transposition ciphers have to offer. Don't be shy about trying your own variations. Always work with your partner, because you will be able to help each other catch problems in your new versions before you put them into your field kit. When you find a system that works for you, write it down in your notebook and keep it for future reference. Remember that a good codemaker can switch from one system to another whenever an adversary might be getting wise to your method. Good luck!

PART 2

Code Breaking

Breaking codes can be the most exciting part of the the spy business. I've saved this section on codebreaking for the end of the field guide because the more practice you have making codes, the more success you'll have breaking codes—and the more you will see the patterns and tendencies in messages written by other codemakers. And that knowledge will be a tremendous help when you have a secret message to crack. Throughout the history of codes and ciphers, a handful of people have been particularly successful in breaking codes and ciphers.

The most important tool you will need to break a cipher is a frequency chart. A **frequency chart** is simply a sheet of paper with the alphabet printed on it. I make my frequency charts on my computer, printing one alphabet down the left-hand margin and another down the center of the page. That way I can cut each sheet in half and get two frequency charts from one sheet of paper.

Now that you have your frequency chart, you're probably wondering what you do with it. You will use this chart to keep count of how many times each letter appears in a message. This is an important part of codebreaking because it can tell you if you are working with a substitution or a transposition cipher. Let me explain.

Certain letters in the English language are used more often than others. Can you guess which letter appears most in English? If you guessed E, you are right. If you guessed T, you were close, because T is the *second* most frequently used letter in English.

The frequency list for English looks like this: **E, T, A, O, N, I, S, R, H, L, D, C, U, F, P, M, W, Y, B, G, V, K, X, Q, J, Z.** I bet it doesn't surprise you that X, Q, J, and Z are the least used letters in English. Since the frequency list will be one of your most important codebreaking tools, I suggest you write it on a file card so it will be at your fingertips and easier to use.

Bear in mind that these frequencies are *averages*, so not every passage you read will follow this chart, especially if it is, say, under two hundred letters. However, the list is accurate enough to use as a starting point when you are trying to break a cipher message. How can it help? If you do a frequency count on an intercepted message and find that the most common letters in it are, let's say, E, T, A, and O, you can bet that your message is a transposition. In other words, the letters in a transposition cipher will follow the English frequency chart. On the other hand, if you see that the most common letters in the message are, let's say, W, B, C, and Q, you can bet that you're looking at a substitution cipher. Further, chances are pretty good that the most frequently used letter in the message is really an E.

It's interesting to note that the most frequently used letters in some other languages are similar to those in English. Here are some examples:

French: E, N, I, R, S
German: E, A, I, S, T
Italian: E, A, I, O, N
Spanish: E, A, O, S, N

Check out these frequency lists:

Most Frequently Used Two-Letter Words

1. of	6. be	11. he	16. if
2. to	7. as	12. by	17. me
3. in	8. at	13. or	18. my
4. it	9. so	14. on	19. up
5. is	10. we	15. do	20. an

Most Frequently Used Three-Letter Words

1. the	6. not	11. our	16. can
2. and	7. had	12. out	17. day
3. for	8. her	13. you	18. get
4. are	9. was	14. all	19. has
5. but	10. one	15. any	20. him

Most Frequently Used Four-Letter Words

1. that	6. your	11. been	16. very
2. with	7. from	12. good	17. when
3. have	8. they	13. much	18. come
4. this	9. know	14. some	19. here
5. will	10. want	15. time	20. just

Most Frequently Used First Letters

T, O, A, W, B, C, D, S, F, M, R, H, I, Y, E, G, L, N, P, U, J, K

Most Frequently Used Last Letters

E, S, T, D, N, R, Y, F, L, O, G, H, A, M, P, U, W

Most Common Double Letters

SS, EE, TT, FF, LL, MM, OO

Now that you know about letter frequency and what it can tell you about a cipher text, let me show you how you can decipher a secret message. Here is a message that your best agent has intercepted and handed over to you to break:

DRO WKZ SC SX NKXQOB. WOOD DRO

KQOXD DYNKI KD DGY SX PBYXD YP

CDYBO. LO BOKNI DY VOKFO.

Read on and we'll solve this mystery together.

The first thing to do is make a frequency chart for this message to see which letters are used more than others. Every time I see a letter in the message, I make a mark next to that letter on my frequency chart. Like this:

You can see from the chart that O appears eleven times, more than any other letter. The next most frequent letter is D, which appears 10 times. So, based on the letter frequencies in English, we make our first educated guess by saying that O = E and D = T. Now we need to plug in those letters and see if we notice any patterns or familiar words. To do that, print your enciphered message, leaving space between lines for writing your deductions. I suggest that you write your cipher text in one color of ink and your plaintext in a different color to avoid confusion. Another good idea, for your reference as you're working, is to write out a plaintext alphabet in one color of ink and, with a different color of ink, write in the cipher letters as you discover them.

So, let's see what we have when we plug in the two letters that we think we know:

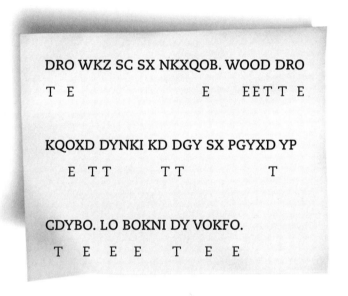

DRO WKZ SC SX NKXQOB. WOOD DRO
T E   E   EET T E

KQOXD DYNKI KD DGY SX PGYXD YP
   E T T   T T   T

CDYBO. LO BOKNI DY VOKFO.
T   E   E   E   T   E   E

It looks like my guesses were pretty good. Now I notice two things:

1. In the three-letter combination of DRO, which appears twice in the message, we think that the first letter is really T and the last letter is E. I can, therefore, be pretty certain that the middle letter, R, is really H, giving us THE. So, one of the things I will do next is plug in H's for the two R's.

2. We've guessed that the last three letters in the first word of the second sentence are EET. There are not many English words with that combination that will fit in this situation. BEET and FEET don't seem to fit, but MEET is a logical choice since we suspect that the next word is THE. So, I will plug in M's for the two W's in the message.

When I have plugged in my latest discoveries, my message now looks like this:

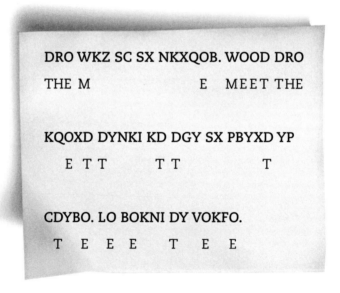

```
DRO WKZ SC SX NKXQOB. WOOD DRO
THE M                E   MEET THE


KQOXD DYNKI KD DGY SX PBYXD YP
  E T T        T T          T


CDYBO. LO BOKNI DY VOKFO.
  T    E   E E    T   E  E
```

Another careful look at the message gives you another letter: Y = O. Can you see that? The key is DY in the last sentence. You know D = T, so you know that Y = O because O is the only letter in English that will make a common word with T: TO. Also, take a look at DGY in the second sentence. You know G = W because W is the only letter in English (other than a repeated O) that will make a common word with T and O: TWO. So, that means you can plug in O's in the six spots where Y appears and a W in the spot where G appears. Now the message looks like this:

DRO WKZ SC SX NKXQOB. WOOD DRO
THE M   E MEET THE

KQOXD DYNKI KD DGY SX PBYXD YP
  T TO   T TWO   O T O

CDYBO. LO BOKNI DY VOKFO.
TO E   E E   TO E   E

This is a good time to remind you that as you figure out the letters in the message, you should be keeping track of which letters you've solved. This is where your plaintext alphabet will come in handy. You can also look at the frequency chart as you go along, to see if you detect any patterns emerging. So far, you've discovered six letters: O = E, D = T, R = H, W = M, Y=O, and G=W.

Now you're ready to take a real chance and see if it pays off. As you look at the frequency chart for this message, you see that the third most common letter is K. Since we know that A is the third most commonly used letter in English, take a chance and say that K = A and hope that the message will reveal more of its secrets when you plug in that letter.

DRO WKZ SC SX NKXQOB. WOOD DRO
THE MA   A   E   MEET THE

KQOXD DYNKI KD DGY SX PBYXD YP
A E T TO A AT TWO   O T O

CDYBO. LO BOKNI DY VOKFO.
  TO E   E EA   TO EA E

This gives us the word AT in the second sentence, along with some plausible-looking letter combinations such as EA. Now let's take a good look at our plaintext alphabet and our cipher equivalents. Try to find a pattern in the letters we've discovered:

cipher: K   O   R   W Y   D G
plaintext: ABCDEFGHIJKLMNOPQRSTUVWXYZ

The letters we have figured out go in order from K to Y (and A to O in the plaintext alphabet), then seem to go to the beginning of the alphabet. And the number of letters *between* letters also looks telling: two (PQ) between O and R, just as there are two (FG) between their equivalents, E and H, in the plaintext alphabet; one (X) between W and Y, just as there is one (N) between M and O in the plaintext alphabet; and so on. If we begin to fill in letters, the pattern becomes clear:

K L M N O P Q R S T U V W X Y Z A B C D E F G H I J
A B C D E F G H I J K L M N O P Q R S T U V W X Y Z

Do you think we've solved the cipher text? Plug the letters into the message and see if we're right:

DRO WKZ SC SX NKXQOB. WOOD DRO
THE MAP IS IN DANGER. MEET THE

KQOXD DYNKI KD DGY SX PBYXD YP
AGENT TODAY AT TWO IN FRONT OF

CDYBO. LO BOKNI DY VOKFO.
STORE. BE READY TO LEAVE.

Before I give you a couple of "intercepted messages" to decipher on your own, I want to offer a couple of suggestions for deciphering a transposition cipher.

Let's suppose the cipher message is

YBAHPD OETIAE UICDNB ANHEDO RGEMCO EWDAOK.

The fact that this message is written in six words of the same length should tell you that this is very likely a transposition cipher. But to confirm our suspicions, make a frequency chart for the message to find out which letters are used more than others.

You will find that the most common letter in the message is E (with five occurrences), followed by A, D, and O (with four occurrences each). While this message is not long enough to have a true frequency distribution, three of the most frequent letters in the message (E, A, and O) happen to be among the four most frequent letters in English. From this we can assume that we are dealing with a transposition cipher. And, for starters, we can also assume that it follows some sort of route.

So, let's see if we can solve this one. The first thing to do is write out the message in a 6 x 6 grid since it contains six six-letter words. Now look at the grid—checking the columns and rows—to see if you can recognize any words.

Once you spot a word, look to see if it is part of a pattern or a route through the grid. Can you find the route? Here's a hint: notice how the first column contains the words YOU ARE. As you look more closely, you will see that it follows the basic route transposition that I explained on pages 57 and 58. Each column, reading from top to bottom, makes up the message: YOU ARE BEING WATCHED. HIDE MAP AND CODEBOOK.

This message follows a basic route, but you need to remember that the letters in the grid could have followed one of many routes. So if the basic route doesn't work, you will have to look for another route. If you still can't see any words to get you heading in the right direction, you should try shifting the rows of letters. Do these steps slowly and carefully, using lots of scrap paper if you need it to try out various guesses. Give your partner and yourself time to study the different configurations of the letters. Don't forget: patience is one of your most important tools when you are trying to break a code.

PRACTICE!

Let's see how well you have learned to break codes. I've helped you out by indicating what type of cipher was used to encode the messages below. Be sure to look back through this section at the frequency charts, as well as at the codemaking examples I used. All of this might help you get going in the right direction. And of course, make sure you have a lot of scrap paper on hand.
Good luck!

SUBSTITUTION CIPHER:

THRPET GDJIT XH HTI. SD CDI GTHI JCIXA NDJ

_____

GTPRW HPUTIN DU UGXTCSH.

_____

TRANSPOSITION CIPHER:

EIS SDT CES AII PND ECE AAO TVF DER AOI WNV
NWE HER.

Answers on page 134.

THE BEALE CIPHER

In 1820 Thomas J. Beale checked into the Washington Hotel in
Lynchburg, Virginia. He turned out to be a friendly man who
stayed the winter at the Washington, but left without a word in
the spring. Two years later Beale return to the Washington and,
once again, he stayed for six months. This time he asked Robert
Morriss, the hotel manager, if he would put Beale's locked strongbox in the hotel safe until he heard from Beale. Morriss obliged,
and in the spring, Beale again left suddenly. Thomas J. Beale was
never seen again.

Morriss did receive one letter from Beale, telling him that if
the hotel manager did not hear from him in ten years, he should
feel free to break the lock on the strongbox and examine the con-
tents. When Morriss opened the box in 1845, he found three
pages of cipher letters and a letter written in a normal manner.
The letter explained that Beale and his friends had had the good
fortune of finding a treasure of gold and silver when they were
prospecting out West. They had brought the treasure to Virginia
and buried it. The cipher message explained exactly where.

Needless to say, Morriss and his friends set out to find the gold and silver. They failed. So did the thousands of other people who have tried to break the Beale cipher since then. The first and third pages remain a mystery. The treasure has never been uncovered. While some people believe the Beale cipher to be a hoax, that has not stopped codebreakers from trying to solve the cipher and find the treasure, which today would be worth about $20 million.

PART 3

CONCEALMENT

As long as people have had secrets, they have developed many ingenious and devious ways of keeping secrets from one another. The ancient Greeks had a word for it: steganography. This term comes from the words *stegano*, meaning "covered," and *graphein*, meaning "to write." Concealment tactics fall into two categories: physically hiding a message in some way and concealing the secret message within another message.

● Early Concealment Techniques

Concealment started with the ancient Greeks. In battles between the two powerful city-states of Athens and Sparta, both sides were always looking for the strategic advantage in battle. Part of that advantage came through good intelligence. But good intelligence doesn't do you much good if you cannot send it and receive it without your enemy finding out your plans should your message be intercepted. So, as they say, necessity was the mother of invention, and several concealment tactics were born.

Herodotus, the ancient Greek historian who became known as the Father of History, tells of one general, Histaiaeus, who used his servants as messengers, but not in the sense of simply carrying a secret message in the usual manner. The general shaved the head of a servant and tattooed the message on his skull. When the servant's hair grew in, he was sent on his way, the message safely concealed beneath a healthy head of hair.

Another master that Herodotus described wasn't nearly as kind to his servants when he wanted to send sensitive military information to his generals. He found a servant who complained of poor eyesight and promised him a solution to his problem. He shaved the slave's head, then *branded* a message on his scalp! When the hair grew in, the master told the servant that his eyesight would be better when he had his head shaved at a camp some miles away.

Another general, Demaratus, who was exiled in Persia, used more humane methods of concealment. He carved a message in a plank of wood, then covered the message with wax. When the wax was melted, the message was revealed.

Aeneas the Tactician, a Greek historian, described an astragal, an ornamental disk, which is believed to have been used as the oldest semagram, an encoding method that doesn't use numbers or letters. The astragal had holes punched in it to represent the letters of the alphabet. To send a secret message, you pull a string through the letters that spell out your message. Anyone who sees this disk would think it was merely a decoration. But your partner simply unwinds the string, keeping track of the order of the lettered holes that the string passed through.

The Romans, who many people believe gave us the first substitution cipher, also had a few concealment tricks of their own. Tacitus, the Roman historian, told of battlefield generals who would dress the wound of an injured soldier with a bandage that contained a secret message. Another trick they used was sewing a message into the sole of a sandal and sending its owner on his way, bearing the secret.

● Null Cipher

One of the most basic ways of concealing a message is to use a **null cipher.** This is a concealment tactic in which only certain letters in a longer message are meaningful. The rest of the letters in the message do a great job of hiding your real message. You can use a perfectly legitimate letter or paragraph to hide your message. Or you can send a list of unrelated words that contain the real message. As you can imagine, this method is more apt to arouse suspicion than if you hid your message in a larger passage that makes sense. For example, here is a meaningless list of words that conceals a message. Can you find it?

SKUNK AVALANCHE VERTICAL EASY YESTERDAY
OCTOBER USUALLY REMOVE SERIOUS
EVERLASTING LAP FOREVER.

Give up? Check the first letter of each word, and you'll find: SAVE YOURSELF. That's my secret message, cleverly hidden in this string of twelve unrelated words.

Of course, there are other ways to hide a message in this fashion. You could use the last letter of each word. Or the second letter. Or you could get fancy and use the third letter of every fourth word. You can hide entire words this way as well by following a predetermined system, like the third word of each sentence. I'm sure you can think up other systems for using a null cipher in a string of words.

PRACTICE!

Why don't you brainstorm a few new null ciphers with your partner and write them down in your notebook. Then actually try to write a message to each other using one of your systems. Be creative. Be clever. Remember, the more your message is concealed from others, the better off you and your partner will be!

THE CIPHER THAT SAVED A LIFE

In the seventeenth century, during England's Civil War, the Puritans captured Sir John Trevanion, a Royalist, and were holding him in a castle in Colchester, a city not too far from London. More than likely, Trevanion was beginning to sweat because he knew that two of his comrades had already made the long walk to the gallows.

Things indeed looked grim for Sir John, when he received a message from a friend:

Worthie Sir John:

Hope, that is ye beste comfort of ye afflicted, cannot much, I fear me, help you now. That I would say to you, is this only: if ever I may be able to requite that I do owe you, stand not upon asking me. 'Tis not much that I can do: but what I can do, bee ye verie sure I wille. I knowe that, if dethe comes, if ordinary men fear it, it frights not you, accounting it for a high honour, to have such a rewarde of your loyalty. Pray yet that you may be spared this soe bitter, cup. I fear not that you will grudge any sufferings; only if bie submissions you can turn them away, 'tis the part of a wise man. Tell me, an if you can, to do for you anythinge that you wolde have done. The general goes back on Wednesday. Restinge your servant to command.

R. T.

Sir John's jailers didn't know who R. T. was—indeed, his identity is lost to history—but they found nothing suspicious in the letter and delivered it to the prisoner. Sir John, however, took immediate relief in the message because he knew a secret message was concealed within the letters of this letter. If you circle the third letter after each punctuation mark—the system agreed upon by Sir John and his friends—you will find the message that pleased the prisoner so much: PANEL AT EAST END OF CHAPEL SLIDES.

Just as no one questioned the letter Sir John received, no one questioned his request to spend time in quiet prayer in the chapel. After an hour, his jailer finally entered the chapel to check on the prisoner. Sir John was long gone through the secret escape panel.

As I've said, you have a better chance of fooling your adversary if you hide your message in legitimate-sounding sentences. For example, if I wanted to conceal SAVE YOURSELF in a sentence that sounds real, I might write SOME ANTIQUE VASES EASILY YELLOW. OTHERS USUALLY RESIST. SOME ENAMELS LAST FOREVER.

One of the oldest examples of the null cipher goes back to the ancient Greeks, when Aeneas punched tiny holes below the letters of his message that were part of a longer letter written on a sheet of parchment. This method of hiding a message survived over the years and wound up in England. At a time when it was very expensive to send a letter but newspapers could be delivered for free, many people would send their personal "letters" by punching pinholes beneath the letters that made up their message in a newspaper article. Other people simply wrote a small dot beneath the letters in the newspaper that made up their message.

You can still use this technique to conceal a secret message. I suggest you use a newspaper or a magazine and simply mark the letters of your message with a pinhole or a small dot from a pen. Your partner will need to know which article in which newspaper you are using, of course, but you might be able to develop a system in which you use a set section of the newspaper on each day of the week.

PRACTICE!

Take a look at your local newspaper and see if you can find seven different sections that can be automatic places to conceal your message with dots. Write them down in your notebook.

● Cardano Grille

One of the most interesting ways to conceal a message is to use a grille, a device that was invented in 1556 by Girolamo Cardano, an Italian doctor and mathematician. (He also created a system of writing for the blind based on touch, nearly 250 years before Louis Braille was born.) A **grille,** or mask, is a card or sheet of paper with windows cut into it. When the grille is placed over a block of letters or words, the letters of your secret message show through the windows. His invention is still referred to as the **Cardano grille,** and with a little patience and practice, you can make one for yourself. Actually, you will want to make a number of them so you can add some variety to the ways you can send secret messages. You can never have too many ways to confuse someone who's trying to break your codes. As you make each grille, put it in your field kit.

To make the first grille, you are going to need some graph paper with fairly large squares along with a pen and an X-Acto knife or scissors. For starters, cut out a piece of graph paper that is about twelve squares high and about fifteen squares wide. (There's nothing special about 12 x 15. Your grille could be 15 x 15 or 20 x 20. Just don't make it too large.) This will be your grille. Next, mark a small x in twelve of the squares. Which ones? That's up to you, but don't cut out any squares in the outer edge of your grille, and leave at least one square between the cutouts.

1. Carefully cut out the squares.
2. Take your grille with the twelve boxes cut out and write a small number (1–12) under each hole. You can number them in any order you want. Skip around. Make it interesting. Your grille should now look something like this:

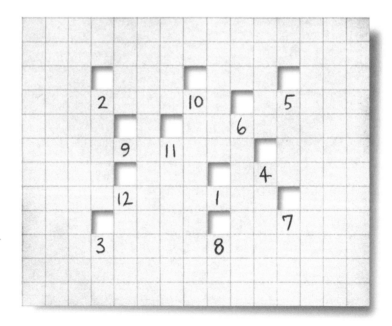

3. Place your grille over a larger piece of graph paper so the holes line up with squares on the graph paper underneath.

4. Using the numbers as a guide, print one letter of this secret message—TRAITORS NEAR—in the twelve holes.

5. Lift your grille. Your message should look something like this:

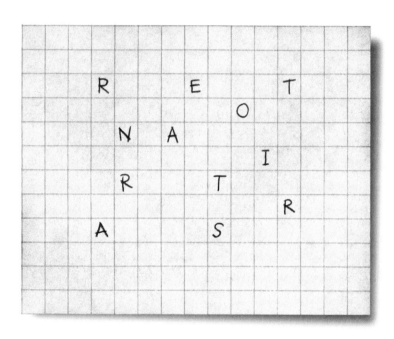

Now comes the concealment part. Fill in all the squares of the 12 x 15 rectangle with letters. Any letters in any order will do. It will look like one of those word-search puzzles.

Or you can simply print letters near and around the letters in your secret message. If you do this, your graph paper will look something like this:

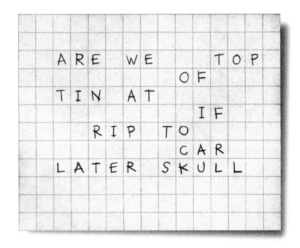

If your message has fewer letters than the number of windows, just fill in the other windows with extra meaningless letters. These letters are called **nulls,** and you can use any letter you want. Just make sure that you put your nulls at the end of the message, otherwise they will confuse your partner.

At this point, you can send your square of letters to your partner. She needs to have an exact copy of your grille, including the numbered sequence of the holes. When she gets your messages, she simply puts her grille over it and copies out in order the letters in the windows. That is your secret message. It's as simple as that.

After you've made a couple of Cardano grilles, you'll probably realize that they work really well with short messages—but what do you do if your message is longer than the number of windows in your grille? Great question! And I've got a great answer: you make a grille that is a bit more advanced. To construct this grille, you will need the same tools and supplies that you used for the first grille. This version is a bit more complicated to use, but with a little patience and practice, you'll be an expert in no time.

To begin, cut out a square of graph paper that is eight squares long on each side—in other words, an 8 x 8 square, which will give you a total of sixty-four smaller squares. Next, number nine squares, marking each one with an arrow. Then carefully cut out a window where each number's arrow is pointing, as shown:

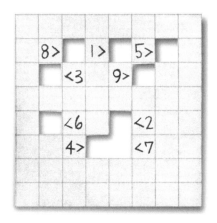

It is *very* important that you number the windows in this way. Any other way might mean that you will not be able to use your grille to send a secret message. Note that it is okay in this type of grille to have windows touching. When you're done, be sure to draw a small mark in your upper left-hand corner, as shown at right.

On another sheet of graph paper, mark off a square that is 8 x 8, the same size as your grille. You can draw a box around it or simply mark off the corners. That box will be where you write your secret message. For practice, let's use this as the message that we want to conceal:

MEET SUPPLY SHIPMENT AT OLD DOCK AT NINE.

Here are the steps that you should follow to use your Cardano grille to write this message:

1. Place your grille over the 8 x 8 square.
2. Write the first nine letters of this message—MEET SUPPL—in the nine windows, starting with window 1 and working your way through window 9. When you lift the grille, your message will look like this:

3. Replace the grille on the paper. Then turn it clockwise a quarter turn. The mark you made in the upper left-hand corner should now be in the upper right-hand corner.

4. When you have made this turn of the grille, write in the next nine letters of your message—Y SHIPMENT—in your windows, starting with window 1 and working your way through to window 9. Your message will now look like this:

5. Turn your grille clockwise again so that the mark is now in the lower right-hand corner. Fill in the next nine letters of your message.

6. Turn your grille a final time. Your mark should now be in the lower left-hand corner. Fill in the rest of the message. Notice that the final segment of the message contains only six letters. That means that you need to fill in the final three spots with nulls. It is best to use letters that you have already used in your message. Letters like

Z, X, and Q might automatically look like nulls to anyone who captures your message and tries to break your code.

I used T, E, and O, three letters that are in my message.

If you have followed my directions, your message should look like a block of thirty-six letters:

When you send your message to your partner, you can simply write out the letters in that order, row by row, which will give you six six-letter words:

NPMMHS EOOLLN AITTTD UESEIY EKTPTO DNAECP

When your partner gets your message, she needs only to print out the letters in order on graph paper, stacking them in a 6 x 6 grid. Then she will place her grille over the block of letters and copy out the letters, nine letters at a time, as she turns the grille after each nine letters. Remember: the grille your partner uses must be an *exact* copy of the one you used, with the same corner marking, or she will not be able to read your message.

● Word Grille

Another way to use a grille for a longer message is to create a **word grille.** It follows the same principal as the Cardano grille, but the word grille has larger rectangular windows in which you write a word instead of just a letter.

For this grille, you will need a 3 x 5 file card. Since you are going to need to cut six windows in that card, I suggest you photocopy the blank card on this page, cut out the windows, then place it over the file card and trace the six windows onto your card.

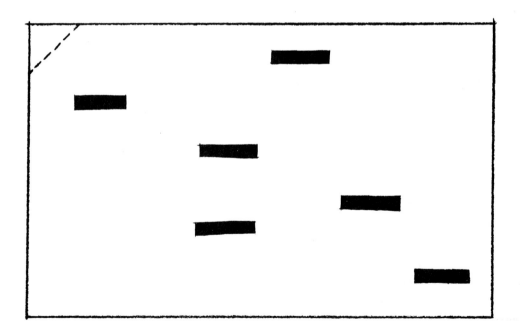

Next, using an X-Acto knife, cut out the six windows in the card and clip off the upper left-hand corner. Do your cutting carefully because if your windows are not where they should be, the grille will not work smoothly.

Let's use this as our secret message: YOUR AGENT IS IN DEEP TROUBLE. STAY AWAY. RETURN TO SAFE HOUSE RIGHT AWAY. WE WILL CONTACT YOU WHEN IT IS SAFE TO ACT. This message has ninety-one letters, so if you used the Cardano grille, you would need to go through three cycles of turns to get in the entire message. But, as you will see, using a word grille can make the process a bit easier because you will only need to flip the grille four times to include all twenty-four words in your message.

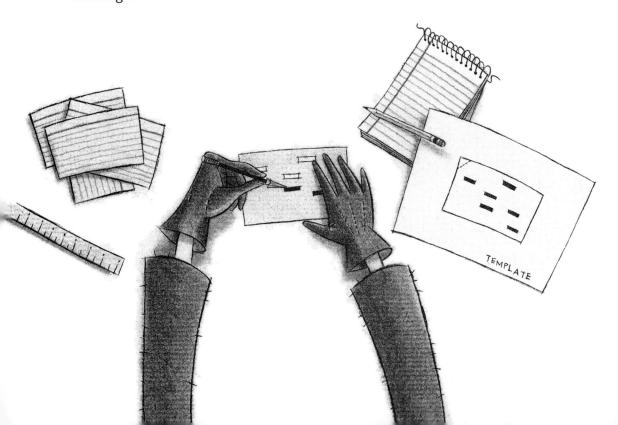

TEMPLATE

First, place your grille over another file card. In each window, write, in order, one of the first six words in your message. Work from top to bottom, as shown below:

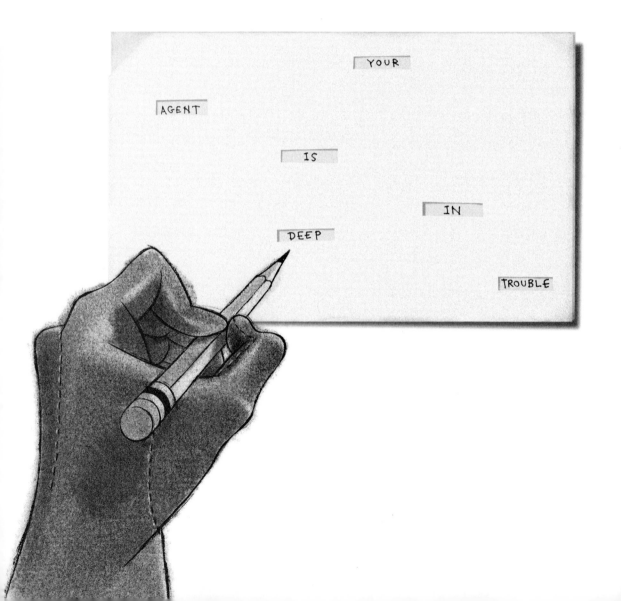

Next, flip the grille so the clipped corner is in the lower left-hand corner. Then write in the next six words of your message just as you wrote the first six words. When you lift your grille, you will see that your card is filling up:

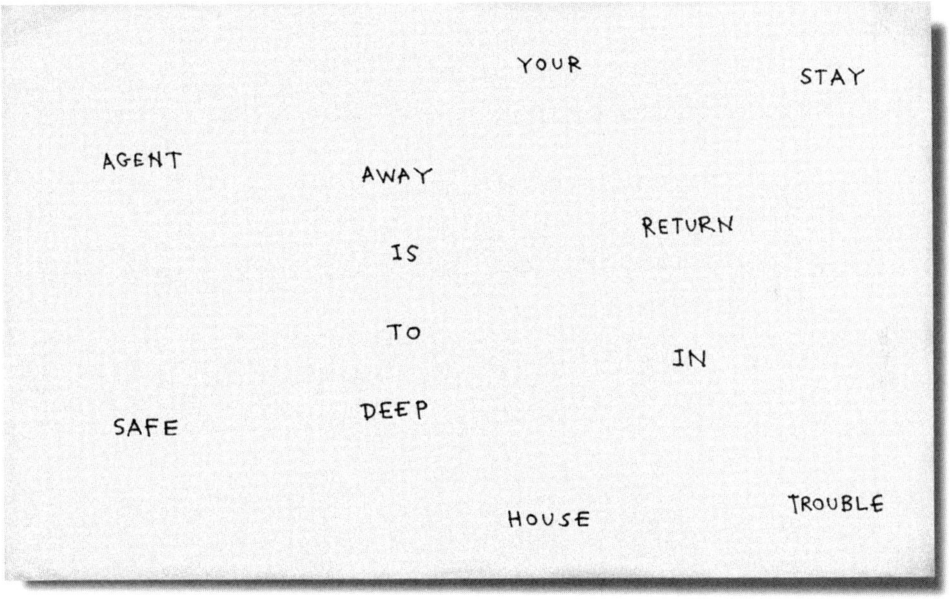

YOUR   STAY

AGENT   AWAY

                        RETURN

        IS

        TO

                    IN

SAFE   DEEP

            HOUSE   TROUBLE

Flip your card so the clipped corner is now in the lower right-hand corner. Write in the next six words of your message. Finally, flip the grille so the clipped corner is in the upper right-hand corner and write in the final six words of the message.

After you have flipped your grille four times and written in all twenty-four words, your bottom card should look like this:

RIGHT   WHEN   YOUR   STAY

AGENT   AWAY   AWAY   IT

WE   IS   IS   RETURN

TO   WILL

SAFE   IN

SAFE   DEEP   TO   CONTACT

ACT   YOU   HOUSE   TROUBLE

It is crucial that you *not* send this card to your partner. If it were to fall into enemy hands, any codebreaker would realize from the pattern of the words that the message was written using a grille. Rather, write out the words, right to left, on another piece of paper or file card and send *that* to your partner. Now if the message is intercepted, all it will reveal is a string of words that make no sense together: RIGHT WHEN YOUR STAY AGENT AWAY AWAY IT WE IS IS RETURN SAFE TO WILL IN SAFE DEEP TO CONTACT ACT YOU HOUSE TROUBLE.

My sample message has exactly twenty-four words so it fits perfectly with four flips of the grille. However, if your message is shorter than twenty-four, simply add nulls, i.e., extra meaning-less words. If your message is longer than twenty-four words, you will need to repeat the process for a second round on a sec-ond file card, or even a third card if your message is very long.

Although the word grille is similar to the Cardano grille, decoding a message written with the word grille is a bit more involved than decoding a message with the Cardano grille. Here are some steps to follow:

1. Place your grille, with the clipped corner in the upper left-hand corner, over a blank card. Draw in the six windows.

2. Flip the grille so the clipped corner is in the lower left-hand corner. Draw in the next six windows.

3. Flip the grille two more times, moving the clipped corner to the lower right-hand corner, then to the upper right-hand corner. Each time you flip the grille, draw in six more windows. When you have finished with four flips, you should have twenty-four windows on your file card that look like this:

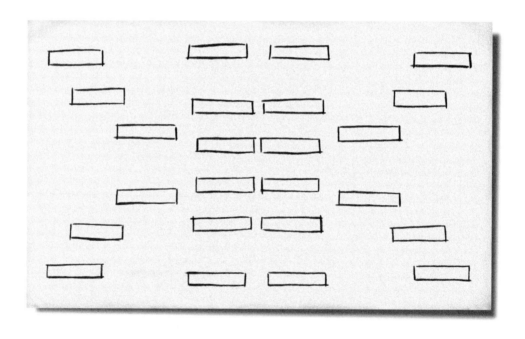

4. Now comes the tricky part. Moving from left to right, top to bottom, write one word of your encoded message in each of the windows that you have drawn. It's important that you write the words in the exact order in which they appear in

the encoded message. (When you read what you've written, it won't make sense. That's okay. Don't worry about it. If you follow directions, everything will work out in the end. Trust me.) When you have written all twenty-four words into the windows, your file card should look like this:

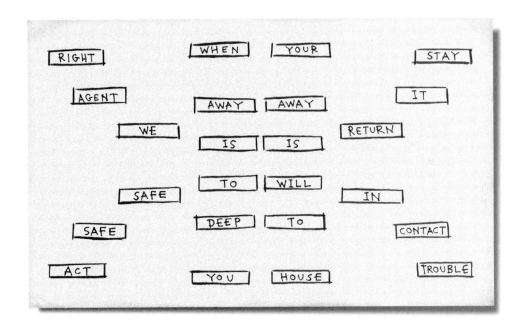

5. Now you can decode this jumble of words with your grille. Place it over the file card, with the clipped corner in the upper left-hand corner. One word will appear in each window. Write those words on a worksheet in your notebook.

6. Flip the grille so the clipped corner is in the lower left-hand corner. Six new words will appear in the windows. Copy them on your worksheet.

7. Flip the grille two more times — to the lower right-hand corner, then the upper right-hand corner — and you will have all twenty-four words in your message in the correct order.

PRACTICE!

Using the word grille card you've made, decipher the message below. If you need help, take a look back at the sequence I described in this section.

Good luck!

WEARING ASK NEW NIGHT AGENT AT A YOU RED WILL FOR NINE THE ARRIVE TIE MEET AT YOU CORRECT SHE TIME WILL ARCADE MONDAY.

Answer on page 134.

Always remember that your partner must know exactly which grille you are using. And if it is a turning grille, she must also know the sequence of turns, i.e., clockwise, counterclockwise, alternating. She must also know the order in which you will write your message. All the examples I have used follow the way we read and write: left to right, top to bottom. But there is nothing to stop you from reversing that, for example, or from writing your message left to right, but bottom to top—so, remember that there are a number of different ways to use the turning grille. Just don't get too complicated. Find a couple of variations that work for you, keep them in your field kit, and stick to them.

● Space Code

One of the simplest concealment tricks is the **space code.** To send a secret message, you simply change the spacing of your message. For example, if I wanted to say ARRIVAL DELAYED BECAUSE OF DANGER, I might use three-letter words: ARR IVA LDE LAY EDB ECA USE OFD ANG ERT (this last letter is a null). Or I could break the message up into two-letter "words" and write it as AR RI VA LD EL AY ED BE CA US EO FD AN GE RT. Just like that, my message has a whole new look.

PRACTICE!

Because it takes a little practice to figure out a space code message that you receive from your partner, let me throw a couple of practice messages your way. The first message is written in the conventional way. The second is a reverse message. Good luck!

1. TR AI NW IL LA RR IV ET ON IG HT AT MI DN IG HT
2. RK FPA ERO ORN STC TWE CTA NTA RCO TFO WAI

Answers on page 134.

Playing Card Code

If you have a short message to send, you can use the **playing card code.** As the name suggests, you need a deck of playing cards for this one. Simply arrange the cards in an order that you and your partner agree on. Then, using a pencil, very lightly print your message along the edge of the deck of cards. When you are finished, shuffle the cards. Your message will disappear. Then leave them in a place where your partner will know to look, like a spot in the library or your clubhouse—when she finds

A variation of the word grille was used in 1777 by Sir Henry Clinton, a general in the British army. He sent a message to General John Burgoyne to let him know of his plans for the upcoming Battle of Saratoga, New York. Here is the message that Clinton sent:

You will have heard, D' Sir I doubt not long before this
can have reached you that Sir W. Howe is gone from hence. The
Rebels imagine that he is gone to the Southward. By this time
however he has filled Chesapeak bay with surprize and terror.
   Washington marched the greatest part of the Rebels to Philadelphia
in order to oppose Sir Wms army. I hear he is now returned upon
finding none of his troops landed but am not sure of this great part
of his troops are returned for certain I am sure this (illegible)
must be vain to them. I am left to command here, half my force may
I am sure defend every thing here with as much safety I shall therefore
send Sir W. 4 or 5 bat" I have too small a force to invade the New England
provinces, they are too weak to make any effectual efforts against me and
you do not want any diversion in your favour I can therefore very well
spare him 1500 men I shall try something certainly towards the close
of the year not till then at any rate. It may be of use to inform you that
report says all yields to you. I own to you that the business
will quickly be over now. S' W's move just at this time has been Capital
Washingtons have been the worst he could take in every respect I
sincerely give you much joy on your success and am with great
sincerity. . . .

This grille is called the *dumbbell cipher* because of the dumbbell shape of the cutout that was placed over the full letter. No one is sure, by the way, if this grille worked. We do know that Burgoyne never acted on the information in the secret message and lost the Battle of Saratoga, a turning point in the war. It is unclear, however, if he ever actually received the message.

the deck of cards, she will arrange the cards in the proper order and easily read the message along the side of the deck. The key here is to write lightly enough so it doesn't attract attention when the cards are shuffled, but dark enough that your partner can read the message when she puts the cards in the proper order. Once she has read the message, she can simply erase the message and your "code machine" is ready for a new message. Why not put a deck of cards in your field kit. It might come in handy one day.

● Dot Cipher

Another method of concealing your secret message is the **dot cipher** and its variants, the line and zigzag ciphers. For this method, you will need some graph paper, a pencil, and a ruler. The message that we will encipher is SHIPMENT ARRIVES TONIGHT.

To begin, you'll need a sheet of graph paper. Draw a margin down the left side of the page, using a ruler as your guide. Then print the alphabet across the top, making sure that the letters line up with the *vertical lines* on the paper. This will be your alphabet key sheet. You can write the alphabet in any order you wish. But, as always, it is important that your partner know the order you are using, and she should create the same key sheet. As long as you have your key sheet in front of you, why don't you print out some other arrangements of the alphabet, skipping five or six lines between each one. You and your partner might even number your alphabets, so you can easily let each other know that you are using alphabet #2, for example, for that day's message.

Here is a sample key sheet, featuring two alphabets you might use.

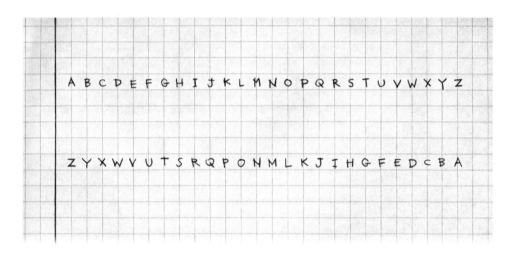

For our example, let's use alphabet #1, which you should write at the top of your key sheet, making sure that the letters line up on the vertical lines on the graph paper. Take a fresh piece of graph paper and draw a margin down the page. Place this on top of your key sheet and below your alphabet, lining up the margins on both pages. Now you are ready to encipher your message. On the first horizontal line under the letter S (the first letter of our message), draw a dot. On the second horizontal line under the letter H, draw a dot. On the third line under the letter I, draw a dot. Moving down the page one line at a time, draw dots for all the letters in our message. When you are finished, your sheet of graph paper should look like this:

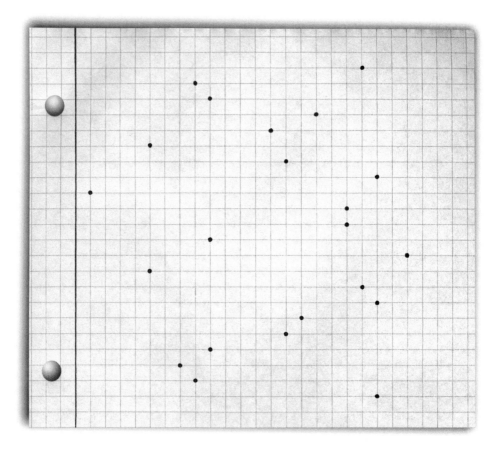

Notice that on the graph paper with the dots, there are no letters written, just dots.

● Line Cipher

If you want to turn your dot cipher into a **line cipher,** simply draw a straight line between *every two dots.* If you do that, your message will now look like this:

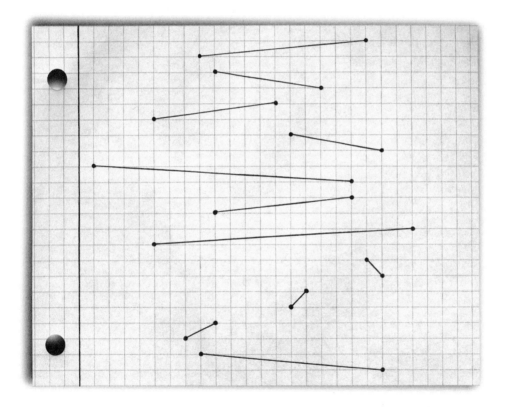

You must draw your lines very carefully because your partner will place the lined sheet over her alphabet key sheet. If your lines are sloppy, they will not line up with the proper letters, and your partner will have a tough time reading your message.

● Zigzag Cipher

If you connected all the dots with lines, it would look like this:

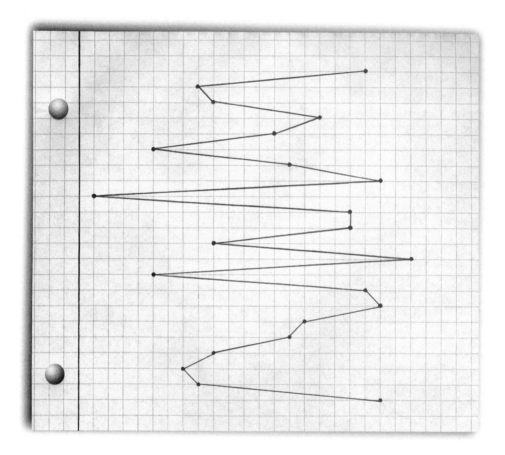

This is called a **zigzag cipher.**

The easiest way to use a dot, line, or zigzag cipher is to pass along the graph paper with your markings to your partner.

If it is too obvious to those who might be watching you to simply give her the paper, you can leave it in a drop that you and she have agreed on. A library is a good place for a drop spot because there are so many places to conceal a sheet of paper. You could, for example, agree to leave it in the current issue of a magazine, in a specified spot in a huge dictionary, or in a particular book on the shelf.

To decipher a message sent using one of these methods, simply place the message sheet over your key sheet, below the alphabet you and your partner have agreed upon. Make sure you've lined up the margins on both sheets. Then slowly move down the message, noting the letter under which each dot appears.

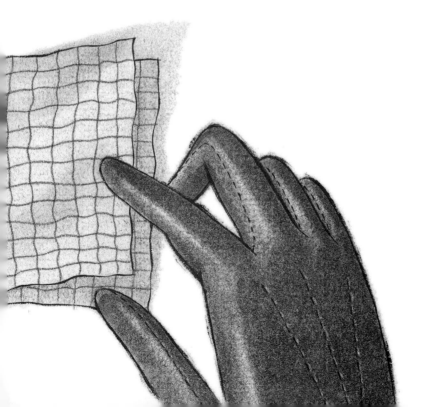

PRACTICE!

See if you can decipher this dot cipher message, using alphabet #1:

Answer on page 134.

Once you've deciphered this message, send your partner a practice message using an alphabet that you have agreed upon. Then meet with her and see how you did making the cipher and how she did deciphering it.

● Invisible Inks

Just like many other code and cipher techniques and systems, the use of **invisible inks** can be traced to ancient times. There are records that the Greeks and the Romans used invisible inks that they extracted from plants and nuts. For example, Pliny the Elder, a Roman naturalist, used the "milk" of the thithymallus plant as an invisible ink. Since then, of course, invisible inks have become more sophisticated, even though they are not nearly as popular as they were during the Middle Ages and the Renaissance. Nevertheless, they have played a part in times of war.

There are two kinds of invisible inks. Some chemicals can be used as invisible inks, but they can be dangerous to use. These chemicals become invisible when they dry. Then they are "developed" with another chemical. This developing chemical is called a reagent, and could be something like iodine vapor or ammonia fumes. The other kind of invisible ink is organic, something easily obtained in nature. Believe it or not, onion juice and vinegar both make good invisible inks. These organic inks are developed by heat.

Before you start concocting your invisible inks, you need to realize that it may take a bit of experimenting before you get the ink so it works just right for you. So be patient as you work.

First of all, you will need some equipment. To write with your ink, you can use a quill (made by cutting the tip off of a feather), toothpicks, or a small brush, the kind you use for model painting or watercolors. While it takes some practice to write with a paintbrush, it does make a good "pen" for invisible ink because it will not leave indentations in the paper, a sure giveaway of your invisible secret. You might want to gather a few small jars to keep your ink in. Baby food jars or 35mm film canisters work well. As far as paper is concerned, you will want a fibrous paper, like school composition paper, rather than glossy paper that won't absorb the ink. All of this equipment can be stored in your field kit.

Once you have your equipment, you can start working on your inks. Here are a few liquids that make good invisible inks.

apple juice

citrus juice (lemon, orange)

onion juice (it might take a few tears to mash enough
    onion to get some ink, but it works well)

vinegar

sugar or honey

salt or Epsom salts

baking soda

As I said, you will need to experiment, particularly with the inks that require you to dissolve something in water. The juice inks may need to be diluted a bit if you can see their color on the paper.

There are other invisible inks. Cola drinks (not diet drinks because it is the sugar that makes the ink work) make good invisible inks if you can dilute them so the brown color doesn't show when you write your message. You can also use a styptic pencil, a sort of crayon that people dab on their skin to cover small nicks they get when they shave. Your mom or dad might have one that you can use.

When you write your message with one of these inks, it will become invisible when it dries. To develop the ink, you need to put some direct heat on the message. You can use a hair dryer, a small heater, an iron on a low setting, or a light bulb, about 150 watts or so. **Be careful when you use heat to develop your message.** You can get burned by any of these heat sources. If you use a light bulb or a heater, keep your message five or six inches away from the heat. Just give the heat time to work. If you iron your message, check constantly to make sure it isn't getting too hot.

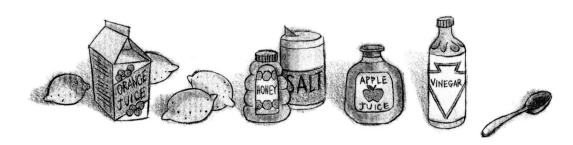

Here are a couple of other invisible ink tricks:

1. You can use milk as an invisible ink. Instead of developing it with heat, rub some ashes across it and the message will appear.

2. Have you ever noticed that when you press down very hard when you are writing with a pencil or pen, you leave indentations in the next sheet of paper? Well, that could be a sort of invisible message, although I would send the sheet that is two or three sheets beneath the one you wrote on. The indentations won't be as obvious. To "develop" such a message, rub the side of a pencil point across the message. You can also shine a light on the paper—slant the light and you should be able to see the message.

3. A message written with starch will be invisible in daylight or electric light, but will become visible when placed under fluorescent light or ultraviolet light. Although fluorescent lights are common, you might need to see if a science teacher can help you find a ultraviolet light at school.

Once you have created your invisible inks, use them in a way that works best for you. One of the drawbacks of invisible ink is that you cannot send a lot of information because you need to find a way to hide all that information. In other words, if you are writing two pages of spy intelligence, you cannot simply send two blank pages. That will immediately draw close examination should it fall into unfriendly hands. Some spies wrote their invisible ink messages between the lines of a real letter. Others wrote the secret messages on the other side of the real letter. You could also put a dot of invisible ink over each letter in a newspaper article that, when taken in order, will spell out your message.

IMPORTANT INFORMATION AHEAD. MEET ME ON NEXT PAGE

CONCEAL TALES OF MENT

During World War II, invisible ink was one of the methods of concealment used by spies. As you might suspect, some of their other methods were quite ingenious. During World War II, intelligence agencies had to be on alert at all times for letters and phone messages that may have included concealed messages. There is evidence of one secret agent who disguised her message as knitting instructions! Another spy, who was watching U.S. Navy activity, cabled his numbers disguised as an order for cigars from a tobacco retailer. He was successful with his concealment until a savvy U.S. agent realized that he was ordering an extraordinary number of cigars. When agents confronted him, he quickly admitted his treachery.

Many secret agents went to great lengths to hide their messages. One spy, who smoked a pipe, developed a pipe that had a secret chamber hidden under the chamber where he put his tobacco. He would hide his message in the secret chamber. But this hiding chamber had its own secret. With a twist of the pipe stem, the inner chamber opened enough for the burning tobacco to ignite the secret message. With a few puffs, the evidence of his secret message went up in smoke!

One of the most ingenious concealments of the war was uncovered in a sweater. A hand-knit sweater was sent by a German spy in England to a prisoner in Germany. Alerted about the sweater, British agents confiscated it and became suspicious of the knots that covered the sweater in no particular order. On a hunch, they unraveled the sweater and saw that the knots appeared at various intervals along the yarn. They suspected that the knots on the sweater stood for letters of the alphabet. Using one knot as a starting point at the base of the wall, they held the yarn against an alphabet printed on the wall and watched how the knots represented letters of a secret message about operations of the Royal Navy.

MAKING A
SECRET-COMPARTMENT BOOK

To make a secret-compartment book, you will need a pencil, an X-Acto knife, and a hardcover book that no one is going to need anymore.

Open the book to page 10 or so. It doesn't matter what page you start on, but it is a good idea to give yourself a "safety zone" of ten or twenty pages. That way, if someone opens the book, he will see the title page and a few normal pages.

When you find a good spot to begin your secret compartment, draw a rectangle on that page to show the size of your hiding place. An opening a little larger than a deck of cards has worked for me. (As a kid, I used a hollowed-out book to keep a decoder ring, a small codebook I'd made, and a brass key. I had no idea which lock the key fit, but that made it much more mysterious.) Keep at least an inch margin all the way around the page. If you get too close to the edge of the page, the pages may fall apart.

Take your X-Acto knife and carefully cut through as many pages as you can without pushing too hard. It is better to take your time and cut fewer pages each time than to try to cut through the whole book in a couple of swipes. With each cut, you will see how your secret compartment grows deeper. With patience and careful cutting, you will soon have a secret compartment that will fool an unsuspecting eye.

SUBJECTS
UNKNOWN

CODEMAKERS and CODEBREAKERS HALL of FAME

The history of secret writing is filled with people whose work with codes and ciphers has been noteworthy in times of war. Here are the stories of some of those figures.

Sir Francis Walsingham left England around 1552 because he disagreed with the religious beliefs of Queen Mary I ("Bloody Mary"). He returned in 1558 when Elizabeth I took the throne and was looking for a spymaster. Francis Walsingham was just that man. He quickly created a spy network that was scattered throughout Europe to gather intelligence for the queen. Perhaps his most famous success was uncovering a plot by Mary Queen of Scots to topple Elizabeth. In fact, it was Walsingham who deciphered Mary's secret messages agreeing to a plan to assassinate Elizabeth.

Benedict Arnold was one of the most courageous soldiers in the Continental army during the American Revolution before he decided to betray the colonies by turning over the important fort of West Point, New York, to the British. Using a book code, he traded many encoded letters with **John André**, the British spymaster in the colonies. After a midnight meeting with Arnold, André was captured while he attempted to return to the British ranks in New York City. Because he was out of uniform, he was tried and convicted of spying. He was hanged in 1780. Arnold escaped to serve in the British army. He spent the rest of his years in London, where he died in 1801.

The **Culper Spy Ring** was one of the most successful spy operations of the American Revolution. The main players were Abraham Woodhull, who lived on Long Island, New York, and Robert Townsend, who lived in New York City. Townsend, using the code name Culper Junior, circulated among the British troops in Manhattan and gathered military intelligence. Using invisible ink, or "stain," as it was called at the time, he sent information to Woodhull, known as Culper Senior, who passed it along to Benjamin Tallmadge, the Continental army's spymaster.

In an attempt to keep the United States from entering World War I, the German foreign minister, Arthur Zimmermann, sent a telegram to the German ambassador in Mexico outlining his plan. The **Zimmermann Telegram** asked that Mexico declare war on the United States. Then, because the United States would need to send troops to defend its southern border from Mexico, it would be unable to commit troops to the war in Europe. British codebreakers cracked the encoded telegram and presented its information to President Wilson. On April 2, 1917, the United States declared war on Germany.

The **Lucy Spy Ring** operated out of Switzerland in World War II on behalf of Russia, Germany's enemy on the Eastern Front. The spy ring got its name from its leader, whose code name was Lucy. The Lucy Spy Ring was successful for a number of reasons. For example, the members of the ring used a number of go-betweens, so the members did not know all the other members in the ring. And when they did meet, the meetings were brief and held in public places, like cafés. For another thing, they knew the other members in the ring only by their code names. When the Nazis realized that the spy ring was operating out of neutral Switzerland, they demanded that the Swiss arrest them. Some members of the spy ring were arrested, but Nazi Germany collapsed before any of them could be convicted of spying.

The **Enigma** was a cipher machine that played an important part in World War II. Created by Germany, the Enigma machine was about the size of a standard typewriter of the day. An agent typed in the message. Electrical impulses generated each time a letter was struck turned one or more of three rotors inside the machine, which enciphered the message in a random manner. It was the codebreakers at Bletchley Park, not far from London, who, after long and hard work, managed to unlock the secret of the Enigma.

The Japanese military had bought an Enigma machine and modified it to create its own code machine, which the American codebreakers called **Purple**. Because the Japanese version of the Enigma had been changed, it was much more difficult to break. Two Americans, Herbert O. Yardley and William Friedman, put together a codebreaking team as skilled as its British counterpart. In fact, Friedman referred to his gang of codebreakers as "magicians." From that nickname came the code name for all the intelligence that came from Purple: Magic.

Some Books to Read

General Histories of Cryptography

The Codebreakers by David Kahn (Scribner, 1967)

The Code Book by Simon Singh (Doubleday, 1999)

About American Codebreakers

The Man Who Broke Purple by Ronald Clark (Little, Brown, 1977)

The American Black Chamber by Herbert O. Yardley

    (Ballantine, 1981)

The American Magic by Ronald Lewin

    (Farrar, Straus and Giroux, 1982)

About British Codebreakers

Seizing the Enigma by David Kahn (Houghton Mifflin, 1991)

The Ultra Secret by F. W. Winterbotham (Harper & Row, 1974)

The Enigma War by Józef Garlinski (Scribner, 1979)

The Zimmermann Telegram by Barbara W. Tuchman

    (Macmillan, 1958)

A Few Final Words

I'm glad that you've read *Top Secret*. Did you build a fat field kit, packed with all kinds of things that can help you become a skilled codemaker and codebreaker? I hope so, because you now have the tools and the knowledge you'll need to make and break codes. Also, I hope you have worked with a friend to make up variations of the codes and ciphers that I have explained in this book. Maybe you have even made up entirely new systems. Good for you! Most of all, I hope that you had fun as you learned about codes, ciphers, and their roles in history.

Before you go off into the world of codes and ciphers, let me offer my last words—encoded, of course, in the book code that I explain on pages 19–20. Using *Top Secret* as your codebook, decipher this message:

0010303 0590805 0862006 1131005 0222109 0531209 0031506

Answer on page 134.

Answer Pages

Page 10: Pictographs

    [CAMPSITE, HOTEL, PARKING, PLAYGROUND]

Page 24: Pig Latin

    [CODE]

    [HAT]

    [WINK]

    [PIG]

    [STUPID]

    ETHAY AMEGAY ILLWAY ARTSTAY ATYAY IXSAY.

Page 28: Caesar Cipher

    1. ABIFSBOV LC PRMMIFBP ABIXVBA.

    2. JBBQ XDBKQ FK COLKQ LC MLPQ LCCFZB.

    1. [REMEMBER TO CHANGE YOUR DISGUISE.]

    2. [A GOOD AGENT KEEPS HER COOL.]

Page 30: St. Cyr Slide

    S VSUO DY GBSDO MSZROBC.

    ZBKMDSMO IYEB MYNOC KXN MSZROBC.

    [CODES HAVE CHANGED HISTORY.]

    [BEWARE OF SPIES.]

Page 33: "Gold Bug" Cipher

[a good glass in the bishop's hostel in the devil's seat—twenty-one degrees and thirteen minutes—northeast and by north—main branch seventh limb east side—shoot from the left eye of the death's-head—a bee-line from the tree through the shot fifty feet out]

Page 33: Dancing Men Cipher

[AM HERE. ABE SLANEY.]

Page 36: Computer Cipher

[SPIES NEED TO BE CAREFUL.]

Page 38: Morse Code

[MORSE CODE IS REALLY A CIPHER.]

Page 40: Modified Semaphore

[A GOOD AGENT USES MANY TOOLS.]

Page 43: Rosicrucian Cipher

[AVOID DANGEROUS SITUATIONS.]

Page 47: Date Shift Cipher

RICGORG TQHZVY MU JXIAX HXT.

Index